曾智明"曾子学术基金"科研成果

山东大学曾子研究所科研成果

曾子研究院科研成果

儒家文明协同创新中心（山东大学）研究成果

曾子文化丛书

《大学》《中庸》通解

通解

Daxue
Zhongyong
Tongjie

曾振宇 主编

段重阳 注译

人民出版社

责任编辑:宫　共
封面设计:胡欣欣

图书在版编目(CIP)数据

《大学》《中庸》通解/曾振宇 主编;段重阳 注译. —北京:人民出版社,
　2023.12
ISBN 978-7-01-026075-4

Ⅰ.①大…　Ⅱ.①曾…②段…　Ⅲ.①《大学》-译文②《中庸》-译文
Ⅳ.①B222.1

中国国家版本馆 CIP 数据核字(2023)第 208423 号

《大学》《中庸》通解
DAXUE ZHONGYONG TONGJIE

曾振宇　主编
段重阳　注译

人 民 出 版 社 出版发行
(100706　北京市东城区隆福寺街 99 号)

北京汇林印务有限公司印刷　新华书店经销

2023 年 12 月第 1 版　2023 年 12 月北京第 1 次印刷
开本:710 毫米×1000 毫米 1/16　印张:5.25　字数:80 千字

ISBN 978-7-01-026075-4　定价:38.00 元

邮购地址 100706　北京市东城区隆福寺街 99 号
人民东方图书销售中心　电话 (010)65250042　65289539

| 曾振宇 |

　　中国著名儒学专家，儒学研究领域"泰山学者"。山东省社会科学名家。山东大学二级教授，山东大学儒学高等研究院教授、博士生导师、史学博士，山东大学儒学高等研究院原副院长、曾子研究院院长。山东省第 9、10、11 届政协委员。美国康涅狄格大学访问学者、布莱恩特大学访问学者。中国哲学史学会曾子研究会会长，国际儒联理事。专业为儒学与中国思想史。

| 段重阳 |

　　陕西耀州人，1993 年 10 月生，华东师范大学中国哲学专业博士，山东大学儒学高等研究院特别资助类博士后，研究方向为儒家哲学。

序 言

"四书"是国学经典。所谓"经典",意味着时间的长河慢慢将文本中有永恒意义的东西筛选出来,并将非本质的成分滤除。简言之,经典永远具有现代性价值。从汉代开始,《论语》便成为人人诵读的蒙学教材。第一部由外国人翻译的《论语》英译本,由拉丁文转译而来,初版于康熙三十年(1691);马歇曼(Joshua Marshman,1768—1837)于1809年出版的《论语》英文节译本,乃第一部直接由中文直译的《论语》英译本;第一部中国人翻译的英译本,则是辜鸿铭于1898出版的译本。迄至今日,"四书"英译本已不下十余种。

不同的哲学与文化形态需要沟通与互鉴。相互学习、"美美与共",各民族历史文化传统中优秀成分才能升华为全世界人人共享的文明成果。在各种英译本"四书"基础上,让全世界各国读者对"四书"的理解有进一步的提升,是本丛书的努力方向,也是本丛书特点所在。我们分别择选出几种有代表性的"四书"译本,从概念、文句和翻译风格等等方面加以比较、分析和点评,冀望读者在阅读过程中,对"四书"的领悟与把握有所深化。譬如,在《论语》一书中,众多弟子问"什么是仁?"孔子的回答都不一致。在大多数语境中,孔子立足于伦理学与工夫论层面讨论"为仁之方",而非逻辑学意义上的"仁是什么?"但是,在逻辑学和道德哲学层面,孔子自己是否对"仁是什么"存在一个哲学的思考和逻辑上的定义？这是我们今天颇感兴趣的话题。实际上，孔子仁论不属于认识论层面的概念，也不仅仅是道德论层面的概念，而应该将其视为审美境界的概念。孔子仁学重心不在于从认识论维度界说"仁是什么"，也不单纯在道德层面表述"应该""如何"，而是更多地关注心与性合一、身与心合一。换言之，天与人合一。这种审美境界的仁学，对外在客观必然性已有所超越，其中蕴含自由与自由意志的色彩。由此而来，也给历代学者如何准确翻译"仁"这一核心概念产生了很大的挑战。理雅各将"仁"译为"true virtue"（真正的美德），辜鸿铭将"仁"译为"moral character"（符合道德的性格）。读者不仅仅是阅读者，也是文本创作者。在阅读作者研究成果的同时，必然提升对"四书"思想的整体认识。

六朝时期的鸠摩罗什曾经感叹道："但改梵为秦，失其藻蔚，虽得大意，殊隔文体。有似嚼饭与人，非徒失味，乃令呕哕也。"①鸠摩罗什的感叹蕴涵诸多困惑与无奈，"依实出华"是译者矻矻以求的奋斗目标，也是阅读者期望之所在。

是为序。

曾振宇
2023 年 7 月 25 日于山东大学

---

① 慧皎撰、汤用彤校注：《高僧传》卷二，中华书局 1992 年版，第 53 页。

目　录

序　言···1

《大学》···1

　　一···1

　　二···4

　　三···7

　　四···7

　　五···8

　　六···11

　　五···12

　　六···14

　　七···16

　　八···17

　　九···18

　　十···21

《中庸》···29

　　第一章···29

　　第二章···33

　　第三章···34

第四章 ……………………………………………………… 34

第五章 ……………………………………………………… 35

第六章 ……………………………………………………… 35

第七章 ……………………………………………………… 36

第八章 ……………………………………………………… 37

第九章 ……………………………………………………… 37

第十章 ……………………………………………………… 38

第十一章 …………………………………………………… 39

第十二章 …………………………………………………… 40

第十三章 …………………………………………………… 42

第十四章 …………………………………………………… 43

第十五章 …………………………………………………… 45

第十六章 …………………………………………………… 46

第十七章 …………………………………………………… 47

第十八章 …………………………………………………… 49

第十九章 …………………………………………………… 51

第二十章 …………………………………………………… 53

第二十一章 ………………………………………………… 62

第二十二章 ………………………………………………… 62

第二十三章 ………………………………………………… 63

第二十四章 ………………………………………………… 64

第二十五章 ………………………………………………… 65

第二十六章 ………………………………………………… 66

第二十七章 ………………………………………………… 68

第二十八章 ………………………………………………… 70

第二十九章 ………………………………………………… 71

第三十章 …………………………………………………… 73

《大学》^[1]

一

【原文】大学^[2]之道，在明明德^[3]，在亲民^[4]，在止于至善^[5]。知止^[6]而后有定^[7]，定而后能静^[8]，静而后能安^[9]，安而后能虑^[10]，虑而后能得^[11]。物有本末，事有终始，知所先后，则近道矣。^[12]

【译文】"大学"用来教导学者修行的途径，在于领会和发挥自己的光明之德，在于亲近和教化民众，在于对最高善的追求。知道最高善之所在，我们就有了确定的目标；有了确定的目标，我们就不会被扰乱；不会被扰乱，我们就能够安于所处之境；安于所处之境，遇事就能够思虑周详；思虑周详，我们就能有所成就。每一物都有根本和枝节，每一件事都有终结和开始，对事物的先后顺序有所把握，就贴近《大学》所教导的修行之途径了。

【英译】What the Great Learning teaches，is—to illustrate illustrious virtue；to renovate the people；and to rest in the highest excellence. The point where to rest being known，the object of pursuit is then determined；and，that being determined，a calm unperturbedness may be attained to. To that calmness there will succeed a tranquil repose. In that repose there may be careful deliberation，and that deliberation will be followed by the attainment of the desired end. Things have their root and their branches. Affairs have their end and their beginning. To know what is first and what is last will lead near to what is taught in the Great Learning.

【注释】

[1]《大学》的英文译文采用理雅各的《大学》英译本（华东师范大学出版社 2010 年影印理雅各编译《中国经典》[*THE CHINESE CLASSICS*]），将该译本同辜鸿铭、林语堂、陈荣捷以及 Roger T.Ames（安乐哲）的英译本进行对比研究。

[2]"大学"有两个含义：其一是教授"穷理、正心、修己、治人之道"的"大人之学"，与教授"洒扫、应对、进退之节，礼乐、射御、书数之文"的"小学"相区别。其二是"太学"，即国家的最高学府。理雅格翻译为"The Great Learning"，辜鸿铭、林语堂翻译为"Higher Education"，陈荣捷翻译为"the Way of learning to be great (or adult education)"。这两种意思在不同的翻译那里有所体现。

[3]"明明德"的第一个"明"是动词，第二个"明"是形容词，意思是使本有的"明德"复现、发挥出来。"明德"意思是"光明的德性"，在《大学》的历代注解中，不同的思想家赋予了其不同的内涵，其中最重要的是"仁义礼智之性"。理雅格翻译为"illustrate illustrious virtue"，辜鸿铭翻译为"bring out the intelligent moral power of our nature"，林语堂翻译为"preserve man's clear character"，陈荣捷翻译为"manifesting the clear character"。林语堂的翻译侧重保持已有的"明德"，其他三位的翻译侧重使"明德"显露、发挥出来。

[4]"亲民"，朱熹解释为"新民"，意思是"革新民众（的德性）"，即教化百姓。王阳明认为"亲民"应该读其本字之音，有"亲近""亲爱""教养"的含义。理雅格翻译为"renovate the people"，辜鸿铭翻译为"make a new and better society (lit. people)"，林语堂翻译为"give new life to the people"，陈荣捷翻译为"loving the people"。陈荣捷的翻译侧重"亲"的含

义，其他三位依据朱熹的解释侧重于"新"的含义。

[5]"止于至善"，按照朱熹的理解，是把握和践行每一事物的必然和当然之理；按照王夫之的理解，是"明德"和"亲民"达到完满之境。理雅格翻译为"rest in the highest excellence"，辜鸿铭翻译为"enable us to abide in the highest excellence"，林语堂翻译为"in dwelling（or resting）in perfecting，or the ultimate good"，陈荣捷翻译为"abiding in the highest good"。四位翻译都保持了"至善"的字面含义。

[6]"知止"，是"知止于至善"的简称。

[7]"定"，朱熹解释为"志有定向"。理雅格翻译为"the object of pursuit is determined"，辜鸿铭翻译为"have a fixed and definite purpose"，林语堂翻译为"have a definite purpose in life"，陈荣捷翻译为"calm"。理雅格、辜鸿铭、林语堂的翻译都突出了朱熹解释中"定"具有的确定人生志向的含义，陈荣捷翻译为"安定"，不取朱熹的解释。

[8]"静"，意思是"不妄动""不扰乱"。理雅格翻译为"calm unperturbedness"，辜鸿铭翻译为"peace and tranquility of mind"，林语堂翻译为"calmness of mind"，陈荣捷翻译为"tranquil"。

[9]"安"，意思是"所处而安""安定于此"。理雅格翻译为"tranquil repose"，辜鸿铭翻译为"peace and serenity of soul"，林语堂、陈荣捷翻译为"peaceful repose"。辜鸿铭的翻译突出了从"mind"到"soul"的深化。

[10]"虑"，意思是"处事精详"，即对事物有所思虑和判断。理雅格翻译为"careful deliberation"，辜鸿铭翻译为"deep，serious thinking and reflection"，林语堂翻译为"think"，陈荣捷翻译为"deliberate"。

[11]"得"，朱熹解释为"得其所止"，即"获得与事物相关的道理"。理雅格翻译为"desired end"，辜鸿铭翻译为"true culture"，林语堂翻译为"knowledge"，陈荣捷翻译为"end"。林语堂的翻译较为贴合朱熹的解释，理雅格和陈荣捷强调了"知止"所开启的目标之实现，而辜鸿铭则是从个人的修身来理解"得"。

[12] 朱熹认为，"本"指的是"明德"，"末"指的是"新民"，"始"指的是"知止"，"终"指的是"能得"。关于"本末"，理雅格翻译为"root and completion"，辜鸿铭翻译为"cause and effects"，林语堂翻译为"foundation and superstructure"，陈荣捷翻译为"roots and branches"。辜鸿铭的翻译突出了因果关系。

二

【原文】古之欲明明德于天下者，先治其国；欲治其国者，先齐其家；欲齐其家者，先修其身；欲修其身者，先正其心；欲正其心者，先诚其意；欲诚其意者，先致其知；致知在格物。[1] 物格而后知至，知至而后意诚，意诚而后心正，心正而后身修，身修而后家齐，家齐而后国治，国治而后天下平。自天子以至于庶人，壹是皆以修身为本。[2] 其本乱而末治者否矣，其所厚者薄，而其所薄者厚，未之有也！

【译文】古代的圣贤想要使得天下之人都能够光大自己的德性，就首先要治理好国家。想要治理好国家，就先要治理好家族；想要治理好家族，先要修养自己的身体；想要修养好自己的身体，先要端正自己的心；想要端正自己的心，先要规范自己的意念；想要规范自己的意念，先要获取相应的知识；获取知识的途径是格物。物格之后才能获取知识，知识获取后才能规范意念，意念规范后才能使心端正，心端正后身体才能得到修养，身体得到修养才能治理好家庭，家族治理好后国家才能得到治理，国家得到治理后天下才能太平。从天子到平民百姓，都是要以修身为根本之事。根本之事没有做好，枝节之事也不可能做好。厚待应该之后做的事情，忽视真正应该做的重要之事，这怎么可以呢！

【英译】The ancients who wished to illustrate illustrious virtue throughout the kingdom，first ordered well their own states. Wishing to order well their states，they first regulated their families. Wishing to regulate their families，they first cultivated their persons. Wishing to cultivate their persons，they first rectified their hearts. Wishing to rectify their hearts，they first sought to be sincere in their thoughts. Wishing to be sincere in their thoughts，they first extended to the utmost their knowledge. Such extension of knowledge lay in the investigation of things. Things being investigated，knowledge became complete. Their knowledge being complete，their thoughts were sincere. Their thoughts being sincere，their hearts were then rectified. Their hearts being rectified，their persons were cultivated. Their persons being cultivated，their families were regulated. Their families being regulated，their states were rightly governed. Their states being rightly governed，the whole kingdom was made tranquil and happy. From the Son of Heaven down to the mass of the people，all must consider the cultivation of the person the root of everything besides. It cannot be，when the root is neglected，that what should spring from it will be well ordered. It never has been the case that what was of great importance has been slightly cared for，and，at the same time，that what was of slight importance has been greatly cared for.

【注释】

[1]"格物、致知、诚意、正心、修身、齐家、治国、平天下"是《大学》的"八条目"。关于"格物致知"，郑玄认为，"知，谓知善恶吉凶之所终始也"，"格，来也。物，犹事也。其知于善深，则来善物；其知于恶深，则来恶物，言事缘人所好来也"。朱熹则把"格物致知"诠释为"即物穷理"："致，推极也。知，犹识也。推极吾之知识，欲其所知无不尽也。格，至也。物，犹事也。穷至事物之理，欲其极处无不到也"。后来王阳明认为"格物致知"就是在每一事物上致良知。

[2] 对于"八条目"（从"平天下"到"格物"），理雅各的翻译是 "make the whole empire peaceful and happy, order State, regulate family, cultivate person, rectify heart, be sincere in thoughts, extend to utmost knowledge, the investigation of things"，辜鸿铭的翻译是 "there be peace and order in the world, secure good government in country, put house in order, order conversation aright, put mind in a proper and well-ordered condition, get true ideas, acquire knowledge and understanding, a systematic study of things"，林语堂的翻译是 "the restoration of peace in the world, order national life, regulate family life, cultivate personal life, set heart right, make will sincere, achieve true knowledge, the investigation of things"，陈荣捷的翻译是 "peace of the world, bring order to state, regulate their family, cultivate their personal lives, rectify their minds, make their wills sincere, extend their knowledge, the investigation of things"，安乐哲的翻译是 "secure peace for the world, effect proper order in state, set family right, cultivate person, become proper in thinking and feeling, resolute in purpose, expand wisdom, understanding how things fit together most productively"。诸家翻译大同小异，其中，安乐哲用 wisdom 取代了 knowledge，并对"格物"做了具体化的解释——"how things fit together"，这与朱子的理解不同，是他对先秦哲学的重新诠释。对"天下"的翻译，world 要比 empire 更加准确。对"国"和"家"的翻译，country、nation 和 state，house 和 family 皆可。对"身"的翻译，除了辜鸿铭外，诸家都采用了 person 的翻译，对其中蕴含的"身体"（body）向度有所忽视，而辜鸿铭使用的 conversation（谈吐）略微轻淡。对于"心"的翻译，heart、mind 皆可，对于"意"的翻译，thoughts、idea、will、purpose 都能表达出其中的意涵，不过根据朱熹的见解，"意"更多指向了处理事物时的具体意念，thoughts 或者 consciousness 更加切合。

三

【原文】康诰曰："克明德。"大甲曰："顾諟天之明命。"[1]帝典曰："克明峻德。"皆自明也。

【译文】《康诰》篇说："能够发扬光明德性。"《太甲》篇说："经常想着这上天赋予的光明之命。"《帝典》篇说："能够彰显你伟大的德性。"这些都是让人们自己知晓自己本身具有的光明德性。

【英译】In the Announcement to Kang，it is said，"He was able to make his virtue illustrious." In the Tai Jia，it is said，"He contemplated and studied the illustrious decrees of Heaven." In the Canon of the Emperor（Yao），it is said，"He was able to make illustrious his lofty virtue." These passages all show how those sovereigns made themselves illustrious.

【注释】

[1] 朱熹说："克，能也"，"顾，谓常目在之也。諟，犹此也，或曰审也。天之明命，即天之所以与我，而我之所以为德者也。常目在之，则无时不明矣"。

四

【原文】汤之盘铭曰："苟日新，日日新，又日新。"康诰曰："作新民。"诗曰："周虽旧邦，其命惟新。"是故君子无所不用其极。[1]

【译文】商汤的沐浴之盘上刻着："如果一天能够洗涤自己，那么每日都要清洗自己，日日都要清洗自己。"《康诰》篇说："作能够日新之民"。《诗经》篇说："周虽然是古老之国，但是它的天命却是新的。"

因此君子需要用尽其力（以自新）。

【英译】On the bathing-tub of Tang，the following words were engraved："If you can one day renovate yourself，do so from day to day. Yea，let there be daily renovation." In the Announcement to Kang，it is said，"To stir up the new people." In the Book of Poetry，it is said，"Although Zhou was an ancient state the ordinance which lighted on it was new." Therefore，the superior man in everything uses his utmost endeavors.

【注释】

[1]"无所不用其极"，郑玄的解释是："极，犹尽也。君子日新其德，常尽心力，不有余也。"朱熹的解释是："自新新民，皆欲止于至善也。"

五

【原文】诗云："邦畿千里，惟民所止。"诗云："缗蛮黄鸟，止于丘隅。"子曰："于止，知其所止，可以人而不如鸟乎！"诗云："穆穆文王，于缉熙敬止！"为人君，止于仁；为人臣，止于敬；为人子，止于孝；为人父，止于慈；与国人交，止于信。[1]诗云："瞻彼淇澳，菉竹猗猗。有斐君子，如切如磋，如琢如磨。瑟兮僩兮，赫兮咺兮。有斐君子，终不可谖兮！"如切如磋者，道学也；如琢如磨者，自修也；瑟兮僩兮者，恂栗也；赫兮喧兮者，威仪也；有斐君子，终不可谖兮者，道盛德至善，民之不能忘也。诗云："於戏前王不忘！"[2]君子贤其贤而亲其亲，小人乐其乐而利其利，此以没世不忘也。[3]

【译文】《诗经》说："王者直接管辖的方圆千里是民众所安居之地。"《诗经》篇："叽叽喳喳的鸟儿栖息在山丘的草木茂盛之地。"孔子说："呜呼！知道自己所应当行动之事，人怎么可以不如鸟呢！"《诗经》

篇说："深远的周文王啊，他持续不断地彰显光明德性并保持在至善之地。"作为君主，要做到仁；作为人臣，要做到敬；作为人子，要做到孝；作为人父，要做到慈；与人们交往，要做到信。《诗经》说："看那淇水的弯曲幽深处，绿竹在茂密地生长。有位文采君子，像制作骨角那样，既要切好，还要磋平；又像雕刻玉石那样，既要雕琢，还要打磨。多么严肃、武毅和盛大啊！这位文采君子，终究令人难以忘记。"诗中所说"像制作骨角那样，既要切好，还要磋"，是说他的学习态度；所说"像雕刻玉石那样，既要雕琢，还要打磨"，是说他的自我修养；所说"严肃、武毅"，是说他战战兢兢、如履薄冰的气象；所谓"盛大"，是说他具有的威严仪态；所谓"这位文采君子，终究令人难以忘记"，是说他德性到了至善的境界，人们永远无法忘记。《诗经》说："呜呼，以前的圣王永远不会被忘记。"君子推崇圣王所推崇的贤者、亲近他们所亲近的人，百姓享受先王遗留下的安乐和利益，因此圣王在去世后也不会被人们遗忘。

【英译】In the Book of Poetry，it is said，"The royal domain of a thousand li is where the people rest." In the Book of Poetry，it is said，"The twittering yellow bird rests on a corner of the mound." The Master said，"When it rests，it knows where to rest. Is it possible that a man should not be equal to this bird?" In the Book of Poetry，it is said，"Profound was King Wen. With how bright and unceasing a feeling of reverence did he regard his resting places！" As a sovereign, he rested in benevolence. As a minister，he rested in reverence. As a son，he rested in filial piety. As a father，he rested in kindness. In communication with his subjects，he rested in good faith. In the Book of Poetry，it is said，"Look at that winding course of the Qi，with the green bamboos so luxuriant！Here is our elegant and accomplished prince！As we cut and then file；as we chisel and then grind：so has he cultivated himself. How grave is he and dignified! How majestic and distinguished! Our elegant and accomplished prince never can be forgotten." That expression— "As we cut and then file," the work of learning. "As we chisel and then grind," indicates that of self-culture. "How grave is he and dignified!" indicates the feeling of cautious reverence. "How commanding and distinguished!" indicates an awe-inspiring deportment. "Our elegant and accomplished prince never can be forgotten," indicates how, when virtue is complete and excellence extreme, the people cannot forget them. In the Book of Poetry, it is said, "Ah! the former kings are not forgotten." Future princes deem worthy what they deemed worthy, and love what they loved. The common people delight in what delighted them, and are benefited by their beneficial arrangements. It is on this account that the former kings, after they have quitted the world, are not forgotten.

【注释】

[1] "止"，朱熹解释为："止，居也，言物各有所当止之处也。""仁、敬、孝、慈、信"，理雅各翻译为"benevolence, reverence, filial piety, kindness, good faith"，辜鸿铭翻译为"love mankind, respect authority, be a dutiful son, be kind to children, be faithful and true"，林语堂翻译为"benevolence, respectfulness, filial piety, kindness, honesty"，陈荣捷翻译为"humanity, reverence, filial piety, deep love, faithfulness"，安乐哲的选本未翻译此句，但在其他地方将"孝"和"慈"翻译为"family reverence"和"maternal commiseration"。其中，辜鸿铭对"敬"的翻译侧重于臣子的政治行为，忽视了"敬"的德性向度。其余诸家翻译大同小异。

[2] "於戏"，"於"在这里一般不简体化为"于"，读音为"呜呼"。

[3] 朱熹说："前王，谓文、武也。君子，谓其后贤后王。小人，谓后民也。此言前王所以新民者止于至善，能使天下后世无一物不得其所，所以

既没世而人思慕之，愈久而不忘也。"

六

【原文】子曰："听讼，吾犹人也，必也使无讼乎！"无情者不得尽其辞。大畏民志，此谓知本。[1]（此谓知本，此谓知之至也。）[2]

【译文】孔子说："处理诉讼，我跟其他人一样，一定要达到没有诉讼的效果！"没有真实情形的不能够说假话。使百姓之心志能够畏服，这才是知道了根本之事。

【英译】The Master said, "In hearing litigations, I am like any other body. What is necessary is to cause the people to have no litigations." So, those who are devoid of principle find it impossible to carry out their speeches, and a great awe would be struck into men's minds; —this is called knowing the root.

【注释】

[1] 对于"无情"和"大畏民志"，郑玄的解释是："情，犹实也。无实者，多虚诞之辞。圣人之听讼，与人同耳，必使民无实者不敢尽其辞，大畏其心志，使诚其意不敢讼。"朱熹的解释是："情，实也。引夫子之言，而言圣人能使无实之人不敢尽其虚诞之辞。盖我之明德既明，自然有以畏服民之心志，故讼不待听而自无也。""大畏民志"是"使民志大畏"的意思，而郑玄所注的古本，关于"诚意"的说明在前，故而说"使诚其意不敢讼"，这也是"知本"的意思，后来王阳明也提倡古本《大学》从而将《大学》之工夫归结为"诚意"而非"格物致知"。王夫之对此也有说明："必使无情者有辞而不得尽，则辞既穷，而情之有无不待辨而自为屈伸，斯无讼矣。而无情者既可有辞矣，何以不得尽也？则所谓'使无讼'也。讼者情虽无而有志，偶有所动，则辞因之以生。故欲止民之争端，必先服其妄志。志欲起而有所畏焉，则欲言之而神以慑，辞不得尽矣。"只有民之志有所畏服，才能

使其呈露"情"之有无。

[2] 郑玄所注古本《大学》此句在"其所厚者薄，而其所薄者厚，未之有也"下。朱熹所注的改本《大学》引程子之言将"此谓知本"句视作衍文，将"此谓知之至也"句视作阙文，故而有"格物补传"。"大畏民志"，理雅各翻译为"a great awe would be struck into men's minds"，辜鸿铭的翻译是"watch with fear and trembling over the hearts of the people"，林语堂翻译为"people are inspired with a great respect or fear（of the magistrate）"，陈荣捷翻译为"a great awe would be struck into people's minds"，安乐哲的选本未翻译此句。辜鸿铭的翻译使得畏惧的主体不再是百姓，与通常的理解不符。

五

【原文】右传之五章，盖释格物、致知之义，而今亡矣。闲尝窃取程子之意以补之曰："所谓致知在格物者，言欲致吾之知，在即物而穷其理也。盖人心之灵莫不有知，而天下之物莫不有理，惟于理有未穷，故其知有不尽也。是以大学始教，必使学者即凡天下之物，莫不因其已知之理而益穷之，以求至乎其极。至于用力之久，而一旦豁然贯通焉，则众物之表里精粗无不到，而吾心之全体大用无不明矣。此谓物格，此谓知之至也。"[1]

【译文】上面第五章应该是解释格物、致知的内涵的，但现在亡佚了。曾经窃取程子的意思以补全："所谓'致知在格物'的意思是说，我如果想要获取知识，就在于在事物中探究它的理。人心之灵，没有不能知的，而天下之物都有各自的理，只是理没有穷尽，所以知识才没有获得。因此《大学》开始教人，必须使学者在天下间的每一个物上，都根据已经知道的理而去探求更多的理，以至于到了它的尽头。当穷理的工夫用力久了后，一旦有豁然贯通，那么众多之物的表面和深层、简单和深奥的理就无所不知了，而我们心的全体大用也就明晓了。这就是

'物格'，这就是'知之至'。"

【英译】The above fifth chapter of the commentary explained the meaning of investigating things and carrying knowledge to the utmost extent，but it is now lost. I have ventured to take the views of the scholar Cheng to supply it，as follows：—The meaning of the expression，'The perfecting of knowledge depends on the investigation of things，'is this：—If we wish to carry our knowledge to the utmost，we must investigate the principles of all things we come into contact with，for the intelligent mind of man is certainly formed to know，and there is not a single thing in which its principles do not inhere. But so long as all principles are not investigated，man's knowledge is incomplete. On this account，the Learning for Adults，at the outset of its lessons，instructs the learner，in regard to all things in the world，to proceed from what knowledge he has of their principles，and pursue his investigation of them，till he reaches the extreme point. After exerting himself in this reaching penetration. Then，the qualities of all things，whether external or internal，the subtle or the coarse，will all be apprehended，and the mind，in its entire substance and its relations to things，will be perfectly intelligent. This is called the investigation of things. This is called the perfection of knowledge.

【注释】

[1] 此段文字不是《礼记·大学》原有的，而是朱熹在重新编排《大学》后自己添入的文字。原本《大学》在"知本"后继之以"诚意"问题，而朱熹将"知之至也"移至"格物补传"之后，又重新编排了一些文字的顺序，形成了从"格物、致知、诚意、正心"的工夫次第。王阳明认为朱熹的改本有问题，《大学》的核心问题是"诚意"，故而以"诚意"为突破口阐发了致良知教，可以参见《大学古本序》和《大学问》。考虑到"四书"的历

史地位，本书采取了朱熹的改本。

六

【原文】所谓诚其意者：毋自欺也，如恶恶臭，如好好色，此之谓自谦，故君子必慎其独也！[1] 小人闲居为不善，无所不至，见君子而后厌然，揜其不善，而着其善。[2] 人之视己，如见其肺肝然，则何益矣。此谓诚于中，形于外，故君子必慎其独也。曾子曰："十目所视，十手所指，其严乎！"富润屋，德润身，心广体胖，故君子必诚其意。[3]

【译文】所谓"诚其意"的意思是：不要自我欺骗，如同厌恶恶臭，如同喜好美色，这就是自慊（自我快足），因此君子必须要做到慎独！小人独处的时候做不善之事毫无顾忌，见到君子之后却隐藏自己，抛弃不善之行，而特意彰显自己的善行。别人看自己，如同看到自己的肝肺那样清楚，这样做又有什么好处呢。这就是在中心做到诚，就能够表现于外部的身体，因此君子必须慎独。曾子说："（一个人独处的时候，）有十只眼睛看着，十只手指着，多么严谨啊！"富贵可以装扮房屋，德性可以修饰身体，心胸广大则身体舒泰，因此君子必须做到诚意。

【英译】What is meant by "making the thoughts sincere" is the allowing no self-deception, as when we hate a bad smell, and as when we love what is beautiful. This is called self-enjoyment. Therefore, the superior man must be watchful over himself when he is alone. There is no evil to which the mean man, dwelling retired, will not proceed, but when he sees a superior man, he instantly tries to disguise himself, concealing his evil, and displaying what is good. The other beholds him, as if he saw his heart and reins；—of what use is his disguise? This is an instance of the saying— "What truly is within will be manifested without." Therefore，the superior man must be watchful over himself when he is alone. The disciple Zeng said，"What ten eyes behold，what ten hands point to，is to be regarded with reverence！" Riches adorn a house，and virtue adorns the person. The mind is expanded，and the body is at ease. Therefore，the superior man must make his thoughts sincere.

【注释】

[1] 关于"自慊"和"慎独"，朱熹解释为："谦，快也，足也。独者，人所不知而己所独知之地也。言欲自脩者知为善以去其恶，则当实用其力，而禁止其自欺。使其恶恶则如恶恶臭，好善则如好好色，皆务决去，而求必得之，以自快足于己，不可徒苟且以殉外而为人也。"郑玄所注古本《大学》，此节在首章"三纲领、八条目"之下。"自慊"，部分版本也做"自谦"，"谦"通"慊"。理雅各翻译为"self-enjoyment"，辜鸿铭翻译为"self-detachment"，林语堂翻译为"satisfy your own conscience"，陈荣捷翻译为"satisfying oneself"，安乐哲翻译为"be unaffected in one's person"。安乐哲的翻译侧重于"不受影响"之义，不免忽视了"自慊"中的自我满足之义。其他诸家翻译皆可。"慎独"，理雅各、林语堂、陈荣捷翻译为"be watchful over himself when（he is）alone"，辜鸿铭翻译为"watch diligently over his secret thought"，安乐哲翻译为"consolidate their virtuosic habits as a resolute disposition for action"。安乐哲的翻译是从慎独的结果来讲，其他人的翻译侧重于慎独的行为本身，更加贴合原文。

[2] 关于"闲居"和"厌然"，朱熹说："闲居，独处也。厌然，消沮闭藏之貌。"

[3] 关于"胖"，郑玄说："胖，犹大也。"朱熹说："胖，安舒也。"

七

【原文】所谓修身在正其心者，身有所忿懥[1]，则不得其正；有所恐惧，则不得其正；有所好乐，则不得其正；有所忧患，则不得其正。心不在焉，视而不见，听而不闻，食而不知其味。此谓修身在正其心。

【译文】所谓"修身在正其心"的意思是，如果心有所愤怒，那么就不得其正；有所恐惧，那么心就不得其正；有所好乐，那么心就不得其正；有所忧患，那么心就不得其正。如果心没有注意到，那么就会视而不见、听而不闻，吃饭也感觉不到味道。这就是修身在于端正自己的心。

【英译】What is meant by, "The cultivation of the person depends on rectifying the mind," may be thus illustrated：—If a man be under the influence of passion he will be incorrect in his conduct. He will be the same, if he is under the influence of terror, or under the influence of fond regard, or under that of sorrow and distress. When the mind is not present, we look and do not see；we hear and do not understand；we eat and do not know the taste of what we eat. This is what is meant by saying that the cultivation of the person depends on the rectifying of the mind.

【注释】

[1] 关于此句，朱熹引程子之言"身有之身当作心"，故而此句及以后几句都是说"心有所忿懥、恐惧、好乐、忧患"。王夫之说："夫经所谓'修身在正其心'者，以心居静而制动，为身之主，而身之用皆自此而起也"，"心与身之相应最速而相合无间也"。

八

【原文】所谓齐其家在修其身者：人之其所亲爱而辟焉，之其所贱恶而辟焉，之其所畏敬而辟焉，之其所哀矜而辟焉，之其所敖惰而辟焉。[1] 故好而知其恶，恶而知其美者，天下鲜矣！故谚有之曰："人莫知其子之恶，莫知其苗之硕。"此谓身不修不可以齐其家。

【译文】所谓"齐其家在修其身"的意思是：人们对于自己所亲近者会更加偏爱，对于自己所轻视者会更加厌恶，对于自己所畏惧者会更加尊敬，对于自己所怜悯者会更加同情，对于自己所傲视者会更加怠慢。因此，喜好一个人却能明白他的缺陷，讨厌一个人却能知道他的优点，这样的人是天下少有的。因此有这样的谚语："（溺爱的）人不知道自己孩子的缺点，（贪得无厌的）不知道自己田地里的苗是健硕的。"因此不修身的话就不能治理好家族。

【英译】What is meant by "The regulation of one's family depends on the cultivation of his person," is this：—Men are partial where they feel affection and love；partial where they despise and dislike；partial where they stand in awe and reverence；partial where they feel sorrow and compassion；partial where they are arrogant and rude. Thus it is that there are few men in the world who love and at the same time know the bad qualities of the object of their love，or who hate and yet know the excellences of the object of their hatred. Hence it is said，in the common adage，"A man does not know the wickedness of his son；he does not know the richness of his growing corn." This is what is meant by saying that if the person be not cultivated，a man cannot regulate his family.

【注释】

[1]"辟"，郑玄本作"譬"，解释为："譬，犹喻也。言适彼而以心度之，曰：吾何以亲爱此人，非以其有德美与？吾何以敖惰此人，非以其志行薄与？反以喻己，则身修与否，可自知也。""譬"在这里是"自我反思"的意思。而朱熹解释为："辟，读为僻"，"辟，犹偏也。五者，在人本有当然之则；然常人之情惟其所向而不加审焉，则必陷于一偏而身不修矣"，指的是缺乏反思和修身的后果。

九

【原文】 所谓治国必先齐其家者，其家不可教而能教人者，无之。故君子不出家而成教于国：孝者，所以事君也；弟者，所以事长也；慈者，所以使众也。康诰曰"如保赤子"，心诚求之，虽不中不远矣。未有学养子而后嫁者也！一家仁，一国兴仁；一家让，一国兴让；一人贪戾，一国作乱；其机如此。此谓一言偾事，一人定国。[1]尧舜帅天下以仁，而民从之；桀纣帅天下以暴，而民从之；其所令反其所好，而民不从。是故君子有诸己而后求诸人，无诸己而后非诸人。所藏乎身不恕，而能喻诸人者，未之有也。故治国在齐其家。诗云："桃之夭夭，其叶蓁蓁；之子于归，宜其家人。"宜其家人，而后可以教国人。诗云："宜兄宜弟。"宜兄宜弟，而后可以教国人。诗云："其仪不忒，正是四国。"其为父子兄弟足法，而后民法之也。此谓治国在齐其家。

【译文】 所谓"治国必先齐其家"的意思是，家族没有治理好而能教化百姓的人是没有的。因此君子不用走出家族就可以教化国中之人：孝可以用来侍奉君主，悌可以用来侍奉长辈，慈可以用来驱使民众。《康诰》里说"如同保持赤子之心"，用心真诚地追求，虽然没有完全实现但也不远了。没有先学会如何养育子女然后才嫁人的。一个家族实现了仁德，一国就能兴起仁德；一个家族实现了谦让，一国就能兴起谦让之风；一人贪戾，那么一国就会作乱，其中的机窍如此。这就是所说的一句话就能败坏事情，一个人就能安定国家。尧舜用仁率领天下，民众跟从他；桀纣用残暴来率领天下，民众也会跟从。如果他的命令跟他的喜好相反，那么民众就不会跟从。因此君子首先要自己做到才能要求别人做到，自己不去做才能责备别人。如果自身内部不符合恕道，却要别人明白这个道理，是没有的事。因此，要治理好国家，就要治理好自己的家族。《诗经》说："桃树长得多么美好，叶子多么茂盛。这个女子出嫁了，善于相处家人。"善于相处家人，才可以教化国人。《诗经》说："善于和兄长、弟弟相处。"善于和兄长、弟弟相处，才可以教化国人。《诗经》说："他的仪态没有差错，可以作为四方各国的表率。"他处在父亲、子女、兄长、弟弟的位置时，都可以作为效法的对象，然后民众才能效法他。这就是治理国家在于治理自己的家族。

【英译】What is meant by "In order rightly to govern the state, it is necessary first to regulate the family," is this：—It is not possible for one to teach others, while he cannot teach his own family. Therefore, the ruler, without going beyond his family, completes the lessons for the state. There is filial piety：—therewith the sovereign should be served. There is fraternal submission：—therewith elders and superiors should be served. There is kindness：—therewith the multitude should be treated. In the Announcement to Kang, it is said, "Act as if you were watching over an infant." If a mother is really anxious about it, though she may not hit exactly the wants of her infant, she will not be far from doing so. There never has been a girl who learned to bring up a child, that she might afterwards marry. From the loving example of one family a whole state becomes loving, and from its courtesies the whole state becomes courteous while, from the ambition and perverseness of the One man, the whole state may be led to rebellious disorder; —such is the nature of the influence. This verifies the saying, "Affairs may be ruined by a single sentence; a kingdom may be settled by its One man." Yao and Shun led on the kingdom with benevolence and the people followed them. Chieh and Chau led on the kingdom with violence, and people followed them. The orders which these issued were contrary to the practices which they loved, and so the people did not follow them. On this account, the ruler must himself be possessed of the good qualities, and then he may require them in the people. He must not have the bad qualities in himself, and then he may require that they shall not be in the people. Never has there been a man, who, not having reference to his own character and wishes in dealing with others, was able effectually to instruct them. Thus we see how the government of the state depends on the regulation of the family. In the Rook of Poetry, it is said, "That peach tree, so delicate and elegant! How luxuriant is its foliage! This girl is going to her husband's house. She will rightly order her household." Let the household be rightly ordered, and then the people of the state may be taught. In the Book of Poetry, it is said, "They can discharge their duties to their elder brothers. They can discharge their duties to their younger brothers." Let the ruler discharge his duties to his elder and younger brothers, and then he may teach the people of the state. In the Book of Poetry, it is said, "In his deportment there is nothing wrong; he rectifies all the people of the state." Yes; when the ruler, as a father, a son, and a brother, is a model, then the people imitate him. This is what is meant by saying, "The government of his kingdom depends on his regulation of the family."

【注释】

[1] 朱熹说："一人，谓君也。机，发动所由也。偾，覆败也。"

十

【原文】所谓平天下在治其国者：上老老而民兴孝，上长长而民兴弟，上恤孤而民不倍，是以君子有絜矩之道也。[1] 所恶于上，毋以使下；所恶于下，毋以事上；所恶于前，毋以先后；所恶于后，毋以从前；所恶于右，毋以交于左；所恶于左，毋以交于右：此之谓絜矩之道。[2]

诗云："乐只君子，民之父母。"民之所好好之，民之所恶恶之，此之谓民之父母。诗云："节彼南山，维石岩岩，赫赫师尹，民具尔瞻。"有国者不可以不慎，辟则为天下僇矣。[3] 诗云："殷之未丧师，克配上帝；仪监于殷，峻命不易。"道得众则得国，失众则失国。是故君子先慎乎德。有德此有人，有人此有土，有土此有财，有财此有用。德者本也，财者末也，外本内末，争民施夺。是故财聚则民散，财散则民聚。是故言悖而出者，亦悖而入；货悖而入者，亦悖而出。

康诰曰："惟命不于常！"道善则得之，不善则失之矣。楚书曰："楚国无以为宝，惟善以为宝。"舅犯曰："亡人无以为宝，仁亲以为宝。"秦誓曰："若有一个臣，断断兮无他技，其心休休焉，其如有容焉。人之有技，若己有之，人之彦圣，其心好之，不啻若自其口出，寔能容之，以能保我子孙黎民，尚亦有利哉。人之有技，媢疾以恶之，人之彦圣，而违之俾不通，寔不能容，以不能保我子孙黎民，亦曰殆哉。"唯仁人放流之，迸诸四夷，不与同中国。此谓唯仁人为能爱人，能恶人。见贤而不能举，举而不能先，命也；见不善而不能退，退而不能远，过也。好人之所恶，恶人之所好，是谓拂人之性，菑必逮夫身。

是故君子有大道，必忠信以得之，骄泰以失之。生财有大道，生之者众，食之者寡，为之者疾，用之者舒，则财恒足矣。仁者以财发身，不仁者以身发财。未有上好仁而下不好义者也，未有好义其事不终者也，未有府库财非其财者也。孟献子曰："畜马乘不察于鸡豚，伐冰之家不畜牛羊，百乘之家不畜聚敛之臣，与其有聚敛之臣，宁有盗臣。"此谓国不以利为利，以义为利也。长国家而务财用者，必自小人矣。彼为善之，小人之使为国家，菑害并至。虽有善者，亦无如之何矣！此谓国不以利为利，以义为利也。

【译文】所谓"平天下在治其国"的意思是：在上位的人孝敬老人，百姓之间就会兴起孝德；在上位的人尊重长辈，百姓就会兴起悌德；在上位的人体恤孤儿，百信就不会背叛，因此君子有絜矩之道。厌恶上位之人的某种行为，就不会要用它来对待下位之人；厌恶下位之人的某种行为，就不会要用它对待上位之人；厌恶前辈的某种行为，就不要用它对待后辈；厌恶后辈的某种行为，就不要用它对待前辈；厌恶右边人的某种行为，就不要用它对待左边的人；厌恶左边人的某种行为，就不要用它对待右边的人，这就是絜矩之道。

《诗经》说："作为民之父母，君子很快乐。"民众所喜好的他就喜好，民众所厌恶的他就厌恶，这就是民之父母。《诗经》说："截然高大的南山啊，山石耸立。赫赫有名的师尹啊，百姓都瞻仰你。"掌管国家之人不可以不谨慎，有一己之偏好就会成为天下的耻辱。《诗经》说："殷商未丧失民众的时候，是可以与上帝相配的。要看到殷商的教训，天命是难以保持的。"这是说，得到百姓的拥护才能拥有国家，失去百姓的拥护就会丧失国家。因此君子先要审慎地修养自身的德性。有了德性才会有百姓，有了百姓才会有土地，有了土地才会有财物，有了财务才会有用度。德是根本，财是末节，以根本为外而以末节为内，是对百姓的掠夺。因此财物聚集起来，民众就会散失，财物散开，民众就会聚集起来。因此君主的命令有违背之处，民众也会以违背之言回复，财货以违背的方式进入君主那里，也会以违背的方式丧失掉。

《康诰》说"天命不是长存的"，是说有善行则得之，不善则失之。《楚书》说："楚国没有什么宝物，只以善为宝物。"舅犯说："逃亡的人没有什么宝物，只有以仁亲为宝物。"《秦誓》说："假如有这样一个臣子，他很诚恳但没有其他技能，他的心地宽厚，能够容纳他人。别人有技能，如同自己拥有，别人有美好的品德，他心里也很喜欢，如同自己说出的。这是能够包容别人，从而能够保护我的子孙黎民，这对我是有利的。别人有技能，就嫉妒和讨厌，别人有美好的品德，就压制阻碍，使其无法与君主沟通。这是不能包容别人的，也就不能保护我的子孙黎民，这对我是有害的。"只有仁者才能够流放这种人，驱逐到四夷之地，不与中国有交往。这就是说，只有仁者能够真正爱人，能够厌恶人。看到贤人而不能举荐，举荐了而不能尽快重用，这是怠慢；看到不善之人不能罢免，罢免后不能使之远离，这就是过错。喜好人们所厌恶的，厌恶人们所喜好的，这就是违逆人性，灾祸必定殃及自身。

因此君子有所行之大道，必须通过忠信而得之，骄横放纵则会失去。生财也有大道：产生财货的人要多，消耗财货的人要少，创造财货的人要勤快，使用财货的人要缓慢，这样财货就能长久足够了。仁者以财货实现自身，不仁者丧失自身而去追求财货。没有在上位的人喜好仁而在下位之人不喜欢义的，没有喜好义却没有将事情进行到底的，没有府库中的财务不是自身之财的。孟献子说："养得起马车的家族不会在乎鸡和猪，有条件保存冰块的家族不会饲养牛羊，拥有百辆车乘的家族不会豢养聚敛财物的家臣，与其有聚敛财物的家臣，不如有盗窃财物的家臣。"这就是说国家不能以财物为利益，而是要以道义为利益。执掌国家却专心于聚敛财用，这必然是受到了小人的引诱。即使执掌国家的人是善良的，但若使用小人治理国家，灾难和祸害就会一起来。虽然有善人，也没有办法。这就是说国家不能以财物为利益，而是要以道义为利益。

【英译】What is meant by "The making the whole kingdom peaceful and happy depends on the government of his State," is this: When the sovereign, behaves to his aged, as the aged should be behaved to, the people become filial; when the sovereign behaves to his elders, as the elders should be behaved to, the people learn brotherly submission; when the sovereign treats compassionately the young and helpless, the people do the same. Thus the ruler has a principle with which, as with a measuring square, he may regulate his conduct. What a man dislikes in his superiors, let him not display in the treatment of his inferiors; what he dislikes in inferiors, let him not display in the service of his superiors; what he hates in those who are before him, let him not therewith precede those who are behind him; what he hates in those who are behind him, let him not therewith follow those who are before him; what he hates to receive on the right, let him not bestow on the left; what he hates to receive on the left, let him not bestow on the right: —this is what is called "The principle with which, as with a measuring square, to regulate one' s conduct."

In the Book of Poetry, it is said, "How much to be rejoiced in are these princes, the parents of the people!" When a prince loves what the people love, and hates what the people hate, then is he what is called the parent of the people. In the Book of Poetry, it is said, "Lofty is that southern hill, with its rugged masses of rocks! Greatly distinguished are you, O grand-teacher Yin, the people all look up to you." Rulers of States may not neglect to be careful. If they deviate to a mean selfishness, they will be a disgrace in the kingdom.In the Book of Poetry, it is said, "Before them sovereigns of the Yin dynasty had lost the hearts of the people, they could appear before God. Take warning from the house of Yin. The great decree is not easily preserved." This shows that, by gaining the people, the kingdom is gained, and, by losing the people, the kingdom is lost. On this account, the ruler will first take pains about his own virtue. Possessing virtue will give him the people. Possessing the people will give the territory. Possessing the territory will give him its wealth. Possessing the wealth, he will have resources for expenditure. Virtue is the root; wealth is the result. If he make the root his secondary object, and the result his primary, he will only wrangle with his people, and teach them rapine. Hence, the accumulation of wealth is the way to scatter the people; and the letting it be scattered among them is the way to collect the people. And hence, the ruler's words going forth contrary to right, will come back to him in the same way, and wealth, gotten by improper ways, will take its departure by the same.

In the Announcement to Kang, it is said, "The decree indeed may not always rest on us;" that is, goodness obtains the decree, and the want of goodness loses it. In the Book of Chu, it is said, "The kingdom of Chu does not consider that to be valuable. It values, instead, its good men." Duke Wen's uncle, Fan, said, "Our fugitive does not account that to be precious. What he considers precious is the affection due to his parent." In the Declaration of the Duke of Qin, it is said, "Let me have but one minister, plain and sincere, not pretending to other abilities, but with a simple, upright, mind; and possessed of generosity, regarding the talents of others as though he himself possessed them, and, where he finds accomplished and perspicacious men, loving them in his heart more than his mouth expresses, and really showing himself able to bear them and employ them: —such a minister will be able to preserve my sons and grandsons and black-haired people, and benefits likewise to the kingdom may well be looked for from him. But if it be his character, when he finds men of ability, to be jealous and hate them; and, when he finds accomplished and perspicacious men, to oppose them and not allow their advancement, showing himself really not able to bear them: — such a minister will not be able to protect my sons and grandsons and people; and may he not also be pronounced dangerous to the State?" It is only the truly virtuous man who can send away such a man and banish him, driving him out among the barbarous tribes around, determined not to dwell along with him in the Middle Kingdom. This is in accordance with the saying, "It is only the truly virtuous man who can love or who can hate others." To see men of worth and not be able to raise them to office; to raise them to office, but not to do so quickly: —this is disrespectful. To see bad men and not be able to remove them; to remove them, but not to do so to a distance: —this is weakness. To love those whom men hate, and to hate those whom men love; —this is to outrage the natural feeling of men. Calamities cannot fail to come down on him who does so.

Thus we see that the sovereign has a great course to pursue. He must show entire self-devotion and sincerity to attain it, and by pride and extravagance he will fail of it. There is a great course also for the production of wealth. Let the producers be many and the consumers few. Let there be activity in the production, and economy in the expenditure. Then the wealth will always be sufficient. The virtuous ruler, by means of his wealth, makes himself more distinguished. The vicious ruler accumulates wealth, at the expense of his life. Never has there been a case of the sovereign loving benevolence, and the people not loving righteousness. Never has there been a case where the people have loved righteousness, and the affairs of the sovereign have not been carried to completion. And never has there been a case where the wealth in such a State, collected in the treasuries and arsenals, did not continue in the sovereign's possession.

The officer Meng Xian said, "He who keeps horses and a carriage does not look after fowls and pigs. The family which keeps its stores of ice does not rear cattle or sheep. So, the house which possesses a hundred chariots should not keep a minister to look out for imposts that he may lay them on the people. Than to have such a minister, it were better for that house to have one who should rob it of its revenues." This is in accordance with the saying: — "In a state, pecuniary gain is not to be considered to be prosperity, but its prosperity will be found in righteousness. " When he who presides over a state or a family makes his revenues his chief business, he must be under the influence of some small, mean man. He may consider this man to be good; but when such a person is employed in the administration of a state or family, calamities from Heaven, and injuries from men, will befall it together, and, though a good man may take his place, he will not be able to remedy the evil. This illustrates again the saying, "In a state, gain is not to be considered prosperity, but its prosperity will be found in righteousness."

【注释】

[1] 关于"倍"，郑玄说："民不倍，不相倍弃也。"朱熹说："倍，与背同。"关于"絜矩"，郑玄说："絜，犹结也，挈也。矩，法也。君子有挈法之道，谓常执而行之，动作不失之。"朱熹说："絜，度也。矩，所以为方

也。……是以君子必当因其所同，推以度物，使彼我之间各得分愿，则上下四旁均齐方正，而天下平矣。"

[2] 朱熹说："此章之义，务在与民同好恶而不专其利，皆推广絜矩之意也。能如是，则亲贤乐利各得其所，而天下平矣。"王夫之对此有这样的说明："家与国不同，而教同也；国与天下不同，而政同也。其教同者，立教之本同也；其政同者，出治之本同也。而政与教不同而理同也。其理同者，人心之顺逆、天理之存亡同也。今即立教于家而教成于国者验之：上尽孝以敬养吾老，一家皆知孝焉，而国之民已动其罔极之思，兴于孝矣；上尽弟以顺承吾长，一家皆知弟焉，而国之民已动其天显之念，兴于弟矣；上尽慈以矜恤夫孤幼，一家皆知慈焉，而国之民已动其恻怛之忧，不倍死以弃生矣。此非家国一理、齐治一心之明效哉？于是而知理有同然而可通，心有同然而必感。""絜矩之道"，理雅各、林语堂、陈荣捷翻译为"the principle, with which, as with a measuring square, to regulate one's conduct"，辜鸿铭翻译为"self-measuring rule"，安乐哲翻译为"way of taking the proper measure of things"，诸家翻译皆可，不过都没有体现出"絜矩之道"所包括的人和我之间在行为上的相感和互联。

[3] 朱熹说："辟，读为僻。僇，与戮同"，"言在上者人所瞻仰，不可不谨。若不能絜矩而好恶殉于一己之偏，则身弑国亡，为天下之大戮矣"。

《中 庸》[1]

第 一 章

【原文】天命之谓性[2]，率性之谓道[3]，修道之谓[4]。道也者，不可须臾离也，可离非道也。是故君子戒慎乎其所不睹，恐惧乎其所不闻。莫见乎隐，莫显乎微，故君子慎其独也。[5]喜怒哀乐之未发，谓之中；发而皆中节，谓之和。中也者，天下之大本也；和也者，天下之达道也。[6]致中和，天地位焉，万物育焉。[7]

【译文】天所给予的是性，遵循自身之性是道，将道立为法度是教。道是须臾不可离开的，能够离开的不是道。因此君子要在不睹不闻之处保持谨慎和敬畏。没有比隐微之处更加昭然明白的了，因此君子需要慎独。喜怒哀乐之情没有发作的时候，叫作"中"；发作后符合节度，叫作"和"。"中"是治理天下的根本，"和"是治理天下的途径。能够实现"中和"，天地万物就会在正当的秩序中发育生长。

【英译】What Heaven has conferred is called The Nature；an accordance with this nature is called The Path of duty；the regulation of this path is called Instruction. The path may not be left for an instant. If it could be left，it would not be the path. On this account，the superior man does not wait till he sees things，to be cautious，nor till he hears things，to be apprehensive. There is nothing more visible than what is secret，and nothing more manifest than what is minute. Therefore the superior man is watchful over himself, when he is alone. While there are no stirrings of pleasure, anger, sorrow, or joy, the mind may be said to be in the state of Equilibrium. When those feelings have been stirred, and they act in their due degree, there ensues what may be called the state of Harmony. This Equilibrium is the great root from which grow all the human actings in the world, and this Harmony is the universal path which they all should pursue. Let the states of equilibrium and harmony exist in perfection, and a happy order will prevail throughout heaven and earth, and all things will be nourished and flourish.

【注释】

[1]《中庸》的英文译文采用理雅各的《中庸》英译本（华东师范大学出版社 2010 年影印理雅各编译《中国经典》[*THE CHINESE CLASSICS*]），将该译本同辜鸿铭、林语堂、陈荣捷以及 Roger T.Ames（安乐哲）、David L.Hall（郝大维）的英译本进行对比研究。

朱熹说："中者，不偏不倚、无过不及之名。庸，平常也。"理雅各、陈荣捷翻译为"the Doctrine of the Mean"，直译是"关于中间 [中道] 的学说"。辜鸿铭翻译为"The Universal Order or Conduct of Life"，直译是"生活的普遍秩序或行为"。林语堂翻译为"Central Harmony"，直译是"中央的 [关键的] 和谐"。安乐哲、郝大维翻译为"focusing the familiar"，直译是"关注熟悉的事物 [切中伦常]"。理雅各、陈荣捷的翻译保持了字面意思，辜鸿铭的翻译对文本进行了进一步解释，林语堂的翻译比较文学化，安乐哲、郝大维也符合"中庸"的含义。因此，理雅各、陈荣捷和安乐哲、郝大维的翻译较为贴切。

[2]"天命"，指"天"之"命"。朱熹说，"命，犹令也"。"天命"就是"天令"。"性"，指人之所为人的依据。朱熹认为"性，即理也"。王阳明认为"性"就是"良知"。王夫之认为是"健顺知能之德"。理雅各、陈荣捷

将"天"翻译为"Heaven"，辜鸿铭、林语堂将"天"翻译为"God"，安乐哲、郝大维直接音译为"Tian"。辜鸿铭和林语堂的翻译有着将"天"人格化的隐忧，这不符合宋明理学乃至中国古代思想的基本倾向，安乐哲、郝大维认为"Heaven"的翻译会带来基督教中上帝创世的隐喻，但"天"就是这个世界本身，因此保留了音译。综合而言，如果翻译的话，"Heaven"比"God"更加适合，其所包含的"sky"含义（《牛津词典》）与"天"之意象有关联，保留音译也是可行的选择。理雅各、林语堂、陈荣捷将"性"翻译为"nature"，辜鸿铭翻译为"law of our being"，安乐哲、郝大维翻译为"natural tendencies"。"nature"有着西方哲学本质主义的语义，而"natural tendencies"则在动态中把握人性，比较符合朱熹"性—情"和"体—用"的哲学思维。

[3]"率"，朱熹解释为"循"，即遵循。"道"，朱熹解释为"当行之路"。理雅各将"道"翻译为"path of duty"，辜鸿铭、林语堂翻译为"moral law"，陈荣捷翻译为"Way"，安乐哲、郝大维翻译为"proper way"。理雅各、辜鸿铭和林语堂的翻译侧重在人间的道德秩序，但《中庸》强调的治理天下有着超出单纯道德领域（duty，moral）的地方，比如礼乐刑政之属，因此宽泛的"Way"更加合适。

[4]"修道"，朱熹解释为"圣人因人物之所当行者而品节之，以为法于天下，则谓之教，若礼、乐、刑、政之属是也"。"修"即"品节"，也就是立法度的意思。王夫之也强调"修道"而立教乃圣人之事。王阳明说："子思性、道、教，皆从本原上说。天命于人，则命便谓之性；率性而行，则性便谓之道；修道而学，则道便谓之教。……圣人率性而行，即是道。圣人以下，未能率性于道，未免有过不及，故须修道。"（《传习录上》）修道是圣人以下的学者之事，也就是致良知教，但与礼乐刑政有别。郑玄说："循性行之，是谓道。脩，治也。治而广之，人放傚之，是曰教。"（郑玄注，王锷点校：《礼记注》，中华书局2021年版，第673页）理雅各将此句翻译为"the regulation of this path is called instruction"，辜鸿铭翻译为"the moral

law when reduced to a system is what we call religion",林语堂翻译为"the cultivation of the moral law is what we call culture",陈荣捷翻译为"cultivating the Way is called education",安乐哲、郝大维翻译为"improving upon this way is called education"。理雅各、辜鸿铭的翻译比较接近朱熹的见解,强调"修道"中的系统之法度。林语堂、陈荣捷和安乐哲、郝大维则强调对"道"本身的修养、修习,更接近于王阳明。从郑玄的注来看,"治而广之,人放傚之"的意思可以容纳二者,而"instruction"的用法过硬、偏向了"指令","教"与"religion"(宗教)有别,考虑到"education"也是培养人的共同途径,朱熹在《大学》中也强调圣人立学校的重要性,因此,第二种翻译更加适合。

[5]"其所不睹""其所不闻",这里的"其"指"君子",也就是君子在独处之时也保持戒慎、恐惧之心,这就是"慎独"。郑玄说:"君子则不然,虽视之无人,听之无声,犹戒慎恐惧自修正,是其不须臾离道。"(《礼记注》,第 674 页)朱熹更进一步,认为"幽暗之中,细微之事,迹虽未形而几则已动,人虽不知而己独知之,则是天下之事无有著见明显而过于此者",哪怕不在独居之时,内心中的想法也只有自己知道,这也需要慎独。"慎独",理雅各、陈荣捷翻译为"watchful over himself when he is alone",辜鸿铭、林语堂翻译为"watches diligently over his secret thoughts",安乐哲、郝大维翻译为"concerned about their uniqueness"。安乐哲、郝大维的译法强调个人的独特性,这不符合古代注疏的通常解释,故而前几种翻译为佳。

[6]"中"与"和",朱熹认为指"性"的"无所偏倚"和"情"的"无所乖戾",而"大本"和"达道"也就是"天命之性"和"循性"。郑玄对此则说:"中为大本者,以其含喜、怒、哀、乐,礼之所由生,政教自此出也。"(《礼记注》,第 674 页)"中"与"和",理雅各、陈荣捷翻译为"equilibrium"(陈荣捷补充了"centrality,mean")与"harmony",辜鸿铭、林语堂翻译为"our true self or moral being"与"moral order"(林语堂也使用了"harmony")。安乐哲、郝大维翻译为"nascent equilibrium"或"focus"

与"harmony"。考虑到"中"与"和"在朱熹的解释中主要用作形容词来指明"性"和"情"，因此"equilibrium"和"harmony"更加合适。

[7]"致、位、育"，朱熹解释为"推而极之、安其所、遂其生"。

第 二 章

【原文】仲尼曰："君子中庸，小人反中庸。[1]君子之中庸也，君子而时中；小人之中庸也，小人而无忌惮也。[2]"

【译文】仲尼（孔子）说："君子能做到中庸，小人不能够做到中庸。君子之所以能做到中庸，是因为君子能够随时随地做到不偏不倚、无过不及；小人之所以不能做到中庸，是因为小人心中无所顾忌。"

【英译】Zhong-ni said, "The superior man embodies the course of the Mean；the mean man acts contrary to the course of the Mean. The superior man's embodying the course of the Mean is because he is a superior man，and so always maintains the Mean. The mean man's acting contrary to the course of the Mean is because he is a mean man，and has no caution."

【注释】

[1]"君子"和"小人"，理雅各翻译为"superior man"和"mean man"，辜鸿铭、林语堂翻译为"moral man"和"vulgar person"，陈荣捷翻译为"superior man"和"inferior man"，安乐哲、郝大维翻译为"exemplary person"和"petty person"。相对于"moral"强调出的道德意味，"superior"和"exemplary"更加贴合文本。

[2]"时中"，朱熹解释为"随时以处中"，即能够在不同的事情中都做到恰到好处，其情皆发而中节。"小人之中庸"，意思是"小人之反中庸"。

第 三 章

【原文】子曰："中庸其至矣乎！民鲜能久矣！"

【译文】孔子说："中庸之道是最高的，民众很少能长久地做到。"

【英译】The Master said，"Perfect is the virtue which is according to the Mean！Rare have they long been among the people，who could practice it！"

第 四 章

【原文】子曰："道之不行也，我知之矣，知者过之，愚者不及也；道之不明也，我知之矣，贤者过之，不肖者不及也。[1]人莫不饮食也，鲜能知味也。[2]"

【译文】孔子说："中庸之道没有实现，我知道其中的原因，智者超出了它，而愚者不及；中庸之道没有明朗，我知道其中的原因，贤者超出它，而不肖者不及。"

【英译】The Master said，"I know how it is that the path of the Mean is not walked in：—The knowing go beyond it，and the stupid do not come up to it. I know how it is that the path of the Mean is not understood：—The men of talents and virtue go beyond it，and the worthless do not come up to it. There is no body but eats and drinks. But they are few who can distinguish flavors."

【注释】

[1] "知者过之，愚者不及"，"知者"通"智者"，朱熹解释说："知者知之过，既以道为不足行；愚者不及知，又不知所以行，此道之所以常不行也。""贤者过之，不肖者不及"，朱熹解释说："贤者行之过，既以道为不足

知；不肖者不及行，又不求所以知，此道之所以常不明也。"朱熹在这里对
"过"和"不及"做了进一步解释，智者和贤者知之过则不足行，行之过则
不足知，愚者和不肖者在知和行两方面皆不及。理雅各、辜鸿铭、林语堂、
陈荣捷都根据朱熹的注解分别用"know"和"do"对"过"和"不及"做
了进一步翻译，安乐哲、郝大维的翻译保留了字面含义。

[2]"人莫不饮食也，鲜能知味也"是用饮食比喻中庸之道的须臾不可
离，但"鲜能知味"也说明大部分人不能在日常生活中把握中庸之道。

第　五　章

【原文】子曰："道其不行矣夫！"

【译文】孔子说："中庸之道没有人践行啊！"

【英译】The Master said，"Alas！How is the path of the Mean
untrodden！"

第　六　章

【原文】子曰："舜其大知也与！舜好问而好察迩言[1]，隐恶而
扬善，执其两端[2]，用其中于民，其斯以为舜乎！"

【译文】孔子说："舜是有大智慧的！舜善于询问，善于体察浅近
的言论，隐藏其中不好的，宣扬其中好的。他把握住两个极端，用其中
不偏不倚的道理治理百姓，他就是这样成为舜的！"

【英译】The Master said，"There was Shun：—He indeed was
greatly wise！Shun loved to question others，and to study their words，
though they might be shallow. He concealed what was bad in them
and displayed what was good. He took hold of their two extremes，
determined the Mean，and employed it in his government of the people.

It was by this that he was Shun！"

【注释】

[1]"迩言"，朱熹认为是"浅近之言"。郑玄说："迩，近也。"理雅各翻译为"shallow"，并认为是周围人之言。辜鸿铭用了"near facts"和"ordinary topics of conversation in everyday life"，陈荣捷用了"ordinary"，安乐哲、郝大维使用了"familiar words"，含义基本一致。

[2]"两端"，朱熹解释为"众论不同之极致"，但认为舜"于善之中又执其两端"；而郑玄认为"两端，过与不及也"。理雅各、陈荣捷用了"extremes"，并确定为"good"与"bad"；辜鸿铭认为是"two extremes of negative and positive"，也指向了"good"与"evil"；安乐哲、郝大维使用了"grasping these ideas at both ends"，具体意蕴则使用了"unhelpful"。他们的翻译基本一致，"两端"都指向了"恶"和"善"，既与朱熹的注释不同，也未使用郑玄的见解。

第 七 章

【原文】子曰："人皆曰予知[1]，驱而纳诸罟擭陷阱之中[2]，而莫之知辟也[3]。人皆曰予知，择乎中庸而不能期月守也。[4]"

【译文】孔子说："人们都说自己是智慧的，但是被驱逐而进入陷阱中却不知道躲避。人们都说自己是智慧的，但选择了中庸之道却不能坚持一个月。"

【英译】The Master said，"Men all say，'We are wise；'but being driven forward and taken in a net，a trap，or a pitfall，they know not how to escape. Men all say，'We are wise；'but happening to choose the course of the Mean，they are not able to keep it for a round month."

【注释】

[1]"予"，我；"知"，通"智"。

[2]"罟攫陷阱"，朱熹解释说："罟，网也；攫，机槛也；陷阱，坑坎也；皆所以掩取禽兽者也。"

[3]"辟"，通"避"。

[4]"期月"，足够一月。

第 八 章

【原文】子曰："回[1]之为人也，择乎中庸，得一善，则拳拳服膺而弗失之矣。[2]"

【译文】孔子说："颜回之为人，选择了中庸之道，拥有了善的事物，就将其坚守在心中不丧失。"

【英译】The Master said "This was the manner of Hui：—he made choice of the Mean，and whenever he got hold of what was good，he clasped it firmly，as if wearing it on his breast，and did not lose it."

【注释】

[1]"回"，即孔子弟子颜回，字子渊。

[2]"拳拳服膺"，朱熹解释为："拳拳，奉持之貌。服，犹着也。膺，胷也。奉持而着之心胷之间，言能守也。""胷"同"胸"。

第 九 章

【原文】子曰："天下国家可均也，爵禄可辞也，白刃可蹈也，中庸不可能也。"[1]

【译文】孔子说："天下、诸国和各家可以得到公平的治理，爵位和俸禄可以辞掉，锋利的刀剑可以踩踏，中庸之道却不可能（轻易）实现。"

【英译】The Master said，"The kingdom，its states，and its families， may be perfectly ruled；dignities and emoluments may be declined；naked weapons may be trampled under the feet；——but the course of the Mean cannot be attained to."

【注释】

[1] "均"，朱熹解释为"平治"。理雅各翻译为"perfectly ruled"，辜鸿铭翻译为"renounce"，林语堂、陈荣捷翻译为"in order"，安乐哲、郝大维翻译为"pacified"。辜鸿铭进一步解释为"to be indifferent to"，即漠视。辜鸿铭的翻译偏离了固有的注疏传统，安乐哲、郝大维的翻译有着"平定"的意思，不如理雅各、林语堂、陈荣捷的翻译强调"治理"更佳。

第 十 章

【原文】 子路问强。子曰："南方之强与？[1]北方之强与？抑而强与？宽柔以教，不报无道，南方之强也，君子居之。衽金革，死而不厌，北方之强也，而强者居之。故君子和而不流，强哉矫！中立而不倚，强哉矫！国有道，不变塞焉，强哉矫！国无道，至死不变，强哉矫！"

【译文】 子路询问如何做到"强大"。孔子说："（你是问）南方的强大，北方的强大，还是你如何做到强大？宽厚温顺地教诲人，不报复不合理的行为，这是南方的强大，君子能够做到。穿着金属制成的盔甲，死亡也不悔恨，这是北方的强大，强者能够做到。因此，君子与众人和谐共处但不失节，这就是强大！坚持不偏不倚，这就是强大！国家有道，不改变穷困时的行为，这就是强大！国家无道，不改变平生的操守，这就是强大！"

【英译】 Zi-lu asked about energy. The Master said, "Do you mean the energy of the South，the energy of the North，or the energy which you should cultivate yourself? To show forbearance and gentleness in teaching others；and not to revenge unreasonable conduct：—this is the energy of Southern regions，and the good man makes it his study. To lie under arms；and meet death without regret：—this is the energy of Northern regions，and the forceful make it their study. Therefore，the superior man cultivates a friendly harmony，without being weak. How firm is he in his energy！ He stands erect in the middle，without inclining to either side. How firm is he in his energy！ When good principles prevail in the government of his country，he does not change from what he was in retirement. How firm is he in his energy！ When bad principles prevail in the country，he maintains his course to death without changing. How firm is he in his energy！"

【注释】

[1] "强"，理雅各、辜鸿铭翻译为 "force of character"，林语堂翻译为 "strength of character"，陈荣捷翻译 "strength"，为安乐哲、郝大维翻译为 "proper strength"，皆可。

第 十 一 章

【原文】 子曰："素隐行怪，后世有述焉，吾弗为之矣。[1]君子遵道而行，半涂而废，吾弗能已矣。君子依乎中庸，遁世不见知而不悔，唯圣者能之。"

【译文】 孔子说："寻求不常见之理、行为怪异，我不去做。君子遵循中庸之道而行，半途而废，我做不到这样。君子依据中庸之道，隐居避世、不被人所知而不后悔，这是只有圣人能做到的。"

【英译】 The Master said，"To live in obscurity，and yet practice wonders，in order to be mentioned with honor in future ages：—this is what I do not do. The good man tries to proceed according to the right path, but when he has gone halfway, he abandons it: —I am not able so to stop. The superior man accords with the course of the Mean. Though he may be all unknown, unregarded by the world, he feels no regret. It is only the sage who is able for this."

【注释】

[1] "素", 是 "索" 字之误, 即 "求索" 之意。朱熹说: "索隐行怪, 言深求隐僻之理, 而过为诡异之行也。然以其足以欺世而盗名, 故后世或有称述之者。" 王夫之认为这里的 "索隐" 并不是指责 "隐僻", 而是批评 "索", 即 "索者, 强相搜求之义"。

第 十 二 章

【原文】 君子之道费而隐。[1]夫妇之愚, 可以与知焉, 及其至也, 虽圣人亦有所不知焉; 夫妇之不肖, 可以能行焉, 及其至也, 虽圣人亦有所不能焉。[2]天地之大也, 人犹有所憾。[3]故君子语大, 天下莫能载焉; 语小, 天下莫能破焉。诗云: "鸢飞戾天, 鱼跃于渊。" 言其上下察也。君子之道, 造端乎夫妇; 及其至也, 察乎天地。

【译文】 君子之道无处不在但又隐蔽。愚笨的夫妇可以知道, 到了极致, 圣人也有所不知; 品行不好的夫妇可以践行, 到了极致, 圣人也有所不能。天地之广大, 人终究有所遗憾。因此君子之道以大而言, 天下没有能承载它的; 以小而言, 天下没有能分裂它的。《诗经》中说: "鸢飞戾天, 鱼跃于渊。" 是说君子之道在天上和地下都很显著。君子之道, 从夫妇处发端, 到了极致, 在天地间也会很显著。

【英译】 The way which the superior man pursues, reaches wide and far, and yet is secret. Common men and women, however ignorant, may intermeddle with the knowledge of it; yet in its utmost reaches，there is that which even the sage does not know. Common men and women，however much below the ordinary standard of character，can carry it into practice；yet in its utmost reaches，there is that which even the sage is not able to carry into practice. Great as heaven and earth are，men still find some things in them with which to be dissatisfied. Thus it is that，were the superior man to speak of his way in all its greatness，nothing in the world would be found able to embrace it，and were he to speak of it in its minuteness，nothing in the world would be found able to split it. It is said in the Book of Poetry，"The hawk flies up to heaven；the fishes leap in the deep." This expresses how this way is seen above and below. The way of the superior man may be found，in its simple elements，in the intercourse of common men and women；but in its utmost reaches，it shines brightly through heaven and earth.

【注释】

[1]　朱熹说："费，用之广也。隐，体之微也。""费"和"隐"，理雅各翻译为"wide and far"和"secret"，辜鸿铭、林语堂翻译为"be found everywhere"和"secret"，陈荣捷翻译为"everywhere"和"hidden"，安乐哲、郝大维翻译为"broad"和"hidden"，皆可。

[2]　朱熹说："君子之道，近自夫妇居室之间，远而至于圣人天地之所不能尽，其大无外，其小无内，可谓费矣。然其理之所以然，则隐而莫之见也。""愚"和"不肖"在这里是强调夫妇的平常。

[3]　"憾"，理雅各、辜鸿铭、林语堂、陈荣捷、安乐哲、郝大维都使用了"satisfy"的否定形式。郑玄说："憾，恨也。"也是遗憾、不满意的意思。

第 十 三 章

【原文】子曰："道不远人。人之为道而远人，不可以为道。诗云：'伐柯伐柯，其则不远。'执柯以伐柯，睨而视之，犹以为远。[1]故君子以人治人，改而止。忠恕违道不远，施诸己而不愿，亦勿施于人。君子之道四，丘未能一焉：所求乎子，以事父未能也；所求乎臣，以事君未能也；所求乎弟，以事兄未能也；所求乎朋友，先施之未能也。庸德之行，庸言之谨，有所不足，不敢不勉，有余不敢尽；言顾行，行顾言，君子胡不慥慥尔！[2]"

【译文】孔子说："道距离人不远。人追求和践履道的时候远离了人，这就不是道了。《诗经》说：'砍伐木料以作斧柄、砍伐木头以作斧柄，它的样式不远。'拿着斧头去砍伐木料，斜着去看，仍然以为很远。所以君子以人自身之道去治理人，直到他改正为止。忠和恕（的行为）离道不远，施加于自己的行为如果不愿意，也不要施加给别人。君子之道有四条，我一个也没做到：要求儿子做到的，我未能对父亲做到；要求臣子做到的，我未能对君主做到；要求弟弟做到的，我未能对兄长做到；要求朋友做到的，我未能先对朋友做到。平常德性的践履，平常言论的谨慎，有所不足的话，不敢不加以勤勉，有所超出的话，也不敢说到了尽头；言论要照顾行为，行为要照顾言论，君子怎么能不笃实呢！"

【英译】The Master said, "The path is not far from man. When men try to pursue a course, which is far from the common indications of consciousness, this course cannot be considered The Path. In the Book of Poetry, it is said, 'In hewing an ax handle, in hewing an ax handle, the pattern is not far off.' We grasp one ax handle to hew the other; and yet, if we look askance from the one to the other, we may consider them as apart. Therefore, the superior man governs men, according to their nature，with what is proper to them，and as soon as they change what is wrong，he stops. When one cultivates to the utmost the principles of his nature，and exercises them on the principle of reciprocity，he is not far from the path. What you do not like when done to yourself，do not do to others. In the way of the superior man there are four things，to not one of which have I as yet attained.— To serve my father，as I would require my son to serve me：to this I have not attained；to serve my prince as I would require my minister to serve me：to this I have not attained；to serve my elder brother as I would require my younger brother to serve me：to this I have not attained；to set the example in behaving to a friend，as I would require him to behave to me：to this I have not attained. Earnest in practicing the ordinary virtues，and careful in speaking about them，if，in his practice，he has anything defective，the superior man dares not but exert himself；and if，in his words，he has any excess，he dares not allow himself such license. Thus his words have respect to his actions，and his actions have respect to his words；is it not just an entire sincerity which marks the superior man?"

【注释】

[1] 朱熹说：“柯，斧柄。则，法也。睨，邪视也。言人执柯伐木以为柯者，彼柯长短之法，在此柯耳。然犹有彼此之别，故伐者视之犹以为远也。”

[2] 朱熹说：“慥慥，笃实貌。”

第 十 四 章

【原文】君子素其位而行，不愿乎其外。[1]素富贵，行乎富贵；

素贫贱，行乎贫贱；素夷狄，行乎夷狄；素患难，行乎患难；君子无入而不自得焉。在上位不陵下，在下位不援上，正己而不求于人则无怨。上不怨天，下不尤人。故君子居易以俟命，小人行险以徼幸。[2]子曰："射有似乎君子；失诸正鹄，反求诸其身。"

【译文】君子根据其所处的地位而行，不羡慕之外的事情。处在富贵之位，就做富贵之位该做的事；处在贫贱之位，就做贫贱之位该做的事；处在夷狄之位，就做夷狄之位该做的事情；处在患难之位，就做患难之位该做的事情；君子在任何环境中都未能不自得。在上位不欺凌下位的人，在下位不攀援上位的人，端正自己而不希求于人，就没有怨恨。上不怨恨天，下不责怪人。因此君子安居于日常生活以等待天命，小人冒险行动而以求不当得之事。孔子说："射箭有类似君子；没有射中目标，反过来探求自己的失误。"

【英译】 The superior man does what is proper to the station in which he is；he does not desire to go beyond this. In a position of wealth and honor，he does what is proper to a position of wealth and honor. In a poor and low position，he does what is proper to a poor and low position. Situated among barbarous tribes，he does what is proper to a situation among barbarous tribes. In a position of sorrow and difficulty，he does what is proper to a position of sorrow and difficulty. The superior man can find himself in no situation in which he is not himself. In a high situation，he does not treat with contempt his inferiors. In a low situation，he does not court the favor of his superiors. He rectifies himself，and seeks for nothing from others，so that he has no dissatisfactions. He does not murmur against Heaven，nor grumble against men. Thus it is that the superior man is quiet and calm，waiting for the appointments of Heaven，while the mean man walks in dangerous paths，looking for lucky occurrences. The Master said，"In archery we have something like the way of the superior man. When the archer misses the center of the target，he turns round and seeks for the cause of his failure in himself."

【注释】

[1] 朱熹说："素，犹见在也。"

[2] 朱熹说："易，平地也。居易，素位而行也。俟命，不愿乎外也。徼，求也。幸，谓所不当得而得者。"郑玄说："易，犹平安也。"

第 十 五 章

【原文】 君子之道，辟如行远必自迩，辟如登高必自卑。诗曰："妻子好合，如鼓瑟琴；兄弟既翕，和乐且耽；宜尔室家；乐尔妻帑。"[1]子曰："父母其顺矣乎!"[2]

【译文】 君子之道，如同向远方旅行必须从近处开始，如同登高山必须从底下处开始。《诗经》中说："能与妻子和合相处，如同鼓瑟弹琴；能与兄弟共处，和乐且满足；安排好你的家室；使得家室合当；与妻子儿女乐处。"孔子说："这样父母就安乐顺心了。"

【英译】 The way of the superior man may be compared to what takes place in traveling，when to go to a distance we must first traverse the space that is near，and in ascending a height，when we must begin from the lower ground. It is said in the Book of Poetry，"Happy union with wife and children is like the music of lutes and harps. When there is concord among brethren，the harmony is delightful and enduring. Thus may you regulate your family，and enjoy the pleasure of your wife and children. " The Master said，"In such a state of things，parents have entire complacence!"

【注释】

[1] 朱熹说：“鼓瑟琴，和也。翕，亦合也。耽，亦乐也。帑，子孙也。”

[2] 顺，郑玄说：“谓其教令行，使室家顺。”

第 十 六 章

【原文】子曰：“鬼神之为德，其盛矣乎！[1]视之而弗见，听之而弗闻，体物而不可遗。使天下之人齐明盛服，以承祭祀。[2]洋洋乎！如在其上，如在其左右。诗曰：‘神之格思，不可度思！矧可射思！’[3]夫微之显，诚之不可揜如此夫。”[4]

【译文】孔子说：“鬼神的德性非常盛大！视之而不见，听之而不闻，每一物都体现了它。使得天下之人，斋戒沐浴，穿上庄重之服来承接祭祀。（鬼神）如同在人们的上方，如同在人们的左右。《诗经》中说：‘神之来，不可测度，何况厌倦呢。’这就是隐微的显现，诚是这样的不可掩盖。”

【英译】The Master said, "How abundantly do spiritual beings display the powers that belong to them! We look for them, but do not see them; we listen to, but do not hear them; yet they enter into all things, and there is nothing without them. They cause all the people in the kingdom to fast and purify themselves, and array themselves in their richest dresses, in order to attend at their sacrifices. Then, like overflowing water, they seem to be over the heads, and on the right and left of their worshippers. It is said in the Book of Poetry, 'The approaches of the spirits, you cannot surmise; and can you treat them with indifference?' Such is the manifestness of what is minute! Such is the impossibility of repressing the outgoings of sincerity!"

【注释】

[1] "鬼神"，理雅各、陈荣捷翻译为"spiritual being"，辜鸿铭、林语堂翻译为"spiritual force"，安乐哲和郝大维翻译为"gods and spirits"。这样的翻译都是将"鬼神"把握为"神灵"或者精神性的东西。但是，朱子说："以二气言，则鬼者阴之灵也，神者阳之灵也。以一气言，则至而伸者为神，反而归者为鬼，其实一物而已。为德，犹言性情功效。"郑玄说："体，犹生也。可，犹所也。不有所遗，言万物无不以鬼神之气生也。"鬼神是气的往复，并非与"物质"对应的"精神"，这里有着中西哲学上的根本差异。

[2] 齐（齊），为"斋"之误。

[3] 朱熹说："格，来也。矧，况也。射，厌也。思，皆声之助，言神之来，其形象不可亿度而知，事之尽敬而已，况可厌倦乎？""思"是语气助词，无意义。

[4] 揜，即"掩"。

第 十 七 章

【原文】子曰："舜其大孝也与！[1]德为圣人，尊为天子，富有四海之内。宗庙飨之，子孙保之。故大德必得其位，必得其禄，必得其名，必得其寿。故天之生物，必因其材而笃焉。故栽者培之，倾者覆之。[2]诗曰：'嘉乐君子，宪宪令德！宜民宜人；受禄于天；保佑命之，自天申之！'故大德者必受命。[3]"

【译文】孔子说："舜是具有大孝的！他的德性是圣人，被尊奉为天子，富有四海，在宗庙中享受供奉，子孙延绵不绝。因此，大德之人必然有地位，必然有财富，必然有声名，必然有长寿。因此天之生物，必然根据其材质而继续如此对待他。因此竖直生长的就培养它，倾倒的就铺盖它，《诗经》中说：'嘉乐君子有显著的德性，善于和百姓相处，接受福禄于天；天保佑他并给予其天命。'因此大德之人必然承受天命。"

【英译】The Master said, "How greatly filial was Shun！ His virtue was that of a sage；his dignity was the throne；his riches were all within the four seas. He offered his sacrifices in his ancestral temple，and his descendants preserved the sacrifices to himself. Therefore having such great virtue，it could not but be that he should obtain the throne，that he should obtain those riches，that he should obtain his fame，that he should attain to his long life. Thus it is that Heaven，in the production of things，is sure to be bountiful to them，according to their qualities. Hence the tree that is flourishing，it nourishes，while that which is ready to fall，it overthrows. In the Book of Poetry，it is said，'The admirable，amiable prince displayed conspicuously his excelling virtue，adjusting his people，and adjusting his officers. Therefore，he received from Heaven his emoluments of dignity. It protected him，assisted him，decreed him the throne；sending from Heaven these favors，as it were repeatedly.' We may say therefore that he who is greatly virtuous will be sure to receive the appointment of Heaven."

【注释】

[1] 关于"孝"，理雅各、陈荣捷、安乐哲和郝大维翻译为 filial (filiality)，辜鸿铭、林语堂翻译为 pious。后者主要是"虔诚"之义，"孝"之德虽然可引申于此，但还是以原意为佳。

[2] 朱熹说："材，质也。笃，厚也。栽，植也。气至而滋息为培。气反而游散则覆。"郑玄说："栽，犹殖也。培，益也。今时人名草木之殖曰栽，筑墙立板亦曰栽。栽，或为'兹'。覆，败也。"

[3] 朱熹说："受命者，受天命为天子也。"

第 十 八 章

【原文】子曰："无忧者其惟文王乎！[1]以王季为父，以武王为子，父作之，子述之。武王缵大王、王季、文王之绪。壹戎衣而有天下，身不失天下之显名。尊为天子[2]，富有四海之内。宗庙飨之，子孙保之。武王末受命[3]，周公成文武之德，追王大王、王季，上祀先公以天子之礼。斯礼也，达乎诸侯大夫，及士庶人[4]。父为大夫，子为士；葬以大夫，祭以士。父为士，子为大夫；葬以士，祭以大夫。期之丧达乎大夫，三年之丧达乎天子，父母之丧无贵贱一也。"

【译文】孔子说："只有周文王才是无忧虑的吧！以王季为父亲，以武王为儿子，父亲开创，儿子继承。武王继续大王、王季、文王的事业，一旦穿上战衣就拥有了天下，也没有失去天下间的美名。尊贵为天子，富有四海之内。在宗庙中享受供奉，子孙延绵不绝。武王年老承受天命，周公实现文王和武王的德业，追奉太王、王季为王，以天子之礼祭祀祖先。这种追封祭祀之礼也在诸侯、大夫以及士人、平民中施行。如果父亲为大夫，儿子为士，父亲死后，应以大夫之礼安葬，用士礼祭祀；如果父亲为士，儿子身为大夫，父亲死后，以士礼安葬，以大夫之礼祭祀。一周年内的丧期之制通行到大夫，三周年的丧期之制通行到天子，为父母服丧，不论身份贵贱，丧期都是一样的。"

【英译】The Master said，"It is only King Wen of whom it can be said that he had no cause for grief！His father was King Ji，and his son was King Wu. His father laid the foundations of his dignity，and his son transmitted it. King Wu continued the enterprise of King Tai，King Ji，and King Wen. He once buckled on his armor，and got possession of the kingdom. He did not lose the distinguished personal reputation which he had throughout the kingdom. His dignity was the royal throne. His riches were the possession of all within the four seas. He offered his sacrifices in his ancestral temple，and his descendants maintained the sacrifices to himself. It was in his old age that King Wu received the appointment to the throne，and the duke of Zhou completed the virtuous course of Wen and Wu. He carried up the title of king to Tai and Ji，and sacrificed to all the former dukes above them with the royal ceremonies. And this rule he extended to the princes of the kingdom，the great officers，the scholars，and the common people. If the father were a great officer and the son a scholar，then the burial was that due to a great officer，and the sacrifice that due to a scholar. If the father were a scholar and the son a great officer，then the burial was that due to a scholar，and the sacrifice that due to a great officer. The one year's mourning was made to extend only to the great，officers，but the three years' mourning extended to the Son of Heaven. In the mourning for a father or mother，he allowed no difference between the noble and the mean."

【注释】

[1] "无忧"，理雅各翻译为 "no cause for grief"，安乐哲、郝大维翻译为 "no grief"，陈荣捷翻译为 "without sorrow"，辜鸿铭、林语堂翻译为 "the most perfect happiness"。若根据原文，理雅各、安乐哲、郝大维、陈荣捷的翻译较为合适，辜鸿铭和林语堂的翻译有脱离文本的缺陷。

[2] "天子"，理雅各翻译为 "imperial throne"，辜鸿铭、林语堂翻译为 "the ruler of the Empire"，陈荣捷翻译为 "the Son of Heaven"，安乐哲、郝大维翻译为 "the Son of tian"。尽管理雅各、辜鸿铭、林语堂的翻译也符合文义，但若考虑到 "天子" 一词有超出单纯的王朝统治者的含义，那么陈荣捷、安乐哲和郝大维的翻译更为合适。

[3] 朱熹说："末，犹老也。"林语堂在此处认为"武王末受命"，应为"文王末受命"，"末"为"未"之误，即周文王未能取代殷商。

[4] "诸侯、大夫、士、庶人"，理雅各翻译为"empire，great officers，scholars，common people"，辜鸿铭、林语堂翻译为"reigning princes，nobles，gentlemen，common people"，陈荣捷翻译为"feudal lords，great officers，officers，the common people"，安乐哲、郝大维翻译为"various vassals，high ministers，scholar-official，common people"，安乐哲、郝大维的翻译更能表现出这四种身份之间的差异。

第 十 九 章

【原文】子曰："武王、周公，其达孝矣乎！孝者，善继人之志，善述人之事者也。春秋修其祖庙，陈其宗器，设其裳衣，荐其时食。宗庙之礼，所以序昭穆也；序爵，所以辨贵贱也；序事，所以辨贤也；旅酬下为上，所以逮贱也；燕毛，所以序齿也。践其位，行其礼，奏其乐，敬其所尊，爱其所亲，事死如事生，事亡如事存，孝之至也。郊社之礼，所以事上帝也，宗庙之礼，所以祀乎其先也。明乎郊社之礼、禘尝之义，治国其如示诸掌乎。"

【译文】孔子说："周武王、周公，他们的确做到了孝！孝是善于继承祖先的志向，善于继承祖先的事业。每逢春秋，修葺祖庙，陈列祖先遗留的重器，布置祖先穿过的衣裳，供奉时令之食。宗庙之礼，是用昭、穆为祖先辨别辈分的；排列爵位，是用来辨别贵贱的；安排祭祀中的职事，是用来辨别贤能的；众人酬饮，下位者敬酒于上，是将礼能够实行于地位卑下者；祭祀之后的燕饮依照发色而排座次，是用以确定年龄大小的。在自己的位置上，进行祭祀之礼，奏响乐曲，敬其所尊崇之人，爱其亲人，侍奉去世的人如同侍奉他在世一样，侍奉亡故的人如同侍奉他活着一样，这就是孝的极致了。郊社之礼，是用来侍奉上帝的，宗庙之礼，是用来祭祀祖先的，知道了郊社之礼和禘、尝之礼的意义，治理国家如同看掌中之物那样容易。"

【英译】The Master said, "How far-extending was the filial piety of King Wu and the duke of Zhou! Now filial piety is seen in the skillful carrying out of the wishes of our forefathers, and the skillful carrying forward of their undertakings. In spring and autumn, they repaired and beautified the temple-halls of their fathers, set forth their ancestral vessels, displayed their various robes, and presented the offerings of the several seasons. By means of the ceremonies of the ancestral temple, they distinguished the royal kindred according to their order of descent. By ordering the parties present according to their rank, they distinguished the more noble and the less. By the arrangement of the services, they made a distinction of talents and worth. In the ceremony of general pledging, the inferiors presented the cup to their superiors, and thus something was given the lowest to do. At the concluding feast, places were given according to the hair, and thus was made the distinction of years. They occupied the places of their forefathers, practiced their ceremonies, and performed their music. They reverenced those whom they honored, and loved those whom they regarded with affection. Thus they served the dead as they would have served them alive; they served the departed as they would have served them had they been continued among them—the height of filial piety. By the ceremonies of the sacrifices to Heaven and Earth they served God, and by the ceremonies of the ancestral temple they sacrificed to their ancestors. He who understands the ceremonies of the sacrifices to Heaven and Earth, and the meaning of the several sacrifices to ancestors, would find the government of a kingdom as easy as to look into his palm！"

第 二 十 章

【原文】哀公问政。子曰："文武之政，布在方策。其人存，则其政举；其人亡，则其政息。人道敏政，地道敏树。夫政也者，蒲卢也。故为政在人，取人以身，修身以道，修道以仁。仁[1]者人也，亲亲为大；义[2]者宜也，尊贤为大；亲亲之杀，尊贤之等，礼所生也。在下位不获乎上，民不可得而治矣！故君子不可以不修身；思修身，不可以不事亲；思事亲，不可以不知人；思知人，不可以不知天。"

天下之达道五，所以行之者三：曰君臣也，父子也，夫妇也，昆弟也，朋友之交也：五者天下之达道也。知、仁、勇三者，天下之达德也，所以行之者一也。[3]或生而知之，或学而知之，或困而知之，及其知之一也；或安而行之，或利而行之，或勉强而行之，及其成功一也。子曰："好学近乎知，力行近乎仁，知耻近乎勇。知斯三者，则知所以修身；知所以修身，则知所以治人；知所以治人，则知所以治天下国家矣。"

凡为天下国家有九经，曰：修身也，尊贤也，亲亲也，敬大臣也，体群臣也，子庶民也，来百工也，柔远人也，怀诸侯也。修身则道立，尊贤则不惑，亲亲则诸父昆弟不怨，敬大臣则不眩，体群臣则士之报礼重，子庶民则百姓劝，来百工则财用足，柔远人则四方归之，怀诸侯则天下畏之。齐明盛服，非礼不动，所以修身也；去谗远色，贱货而贵德，所以劝贤也；尊其位，重其禄，同其好恶，所以劝亲亲也；官盛任使，所以劝大臣也；忠信重禄，所以劝士也；时使薄敛，所以劝百姓也；日省月试，既禀称事，所以劝百工也；送往迎来，嘉善而矜不能，所以柔远人也；继绝世，举废国，治乱持危，朝聘以时，厚往而薄来，所以怀诸侯也。

凡为天下国家有九经，所以行之者一也。凡事豫则立，不豫则废。言前定则不跲，事前定则不困，行前定则不疚，道前定则不穷。在下位不获乎上，民不可得而治矣；获乎上有道：不信乎朋友，不获乎上矣；信乎朋友有道：不顺乎亲，不信乎朋友矣；顺乎亲有道：反诸身不诚，不顺乎亲矣；诚身有道：不明乎善，不诚乎身矣。

诚者，天之道也；诚之者，人之道也。[4]诚者不勉而中，不思而得，从容中道，圣人也。诚之者，择善而固执之者也。博学之，审问之，慎思之，明辨之，笃行之。有弗学，学之弗能弗措也；有弗问，问之弗知弗措也；有弗思，思之弗得弗措也；有弗辨，辨之弗明弗措也；有弗行，行之弗笃弗措也；人一能之己百之，人十能之己千之。果能此道矣，虽愚必明，虽柔必强。

【译文】鲁哀公问如何治理国家。孔子说："周文王和武王治理国家的方式，公布在木板、简册上了。他们活着，那么其政策就能推行，他们去世了，那么其政策就熄灭了。人道（的好坏）能够迅速地在政治中看出来，地道（的好坏）能够迅速地在树木中看出来。政治就如同蒲卢一样。因此，治理国家的关键在选拔贤人，选拔贤人的关键在君主之身，修身的关键在于中庸之道，遵奉中庸之道的关键在于仁。仁以人身而言，以亲近亲人为大；义以适宜而言，以尊奉贤人为大；对亲人之爱的递减、对贤人尊奉的差别，就是礼的起源。在下位的人如果没有获得上位者的任命，就不能治理民众。因此君子不可以不修身；想要修身，不可以不侍奉双亲；想要侍奉双亲，不可以不知道人；想要知道人，不可以不知道天。"

天下有五条共同之道，能够实行的人之德有三种：君臣、父子、夫妇、兄弟、朋友交往之道，是五条共同之道。智、仁、勇，是三种共同之德，行动起来是一致的。有的人生来就知道，有的人学习了才知道，有的人经历了困苦才知道，等到他们都知道了，是一样的；有的人安然地去做，有的人为了利益去做，有的人勉强地去做，等到他们做到了，是一样的。孔子说："喜好学习就接近智慧，努力行动就接近仁，知道羞耻就接近勇。知道这三者，就知道如何修身；知道如何修身，就知道如何治理百姓；知道如何治理百姓，就知道如何治理天下国家了。"

治理天下国家总共有九条原则：修养己身、尊奉贤者、亲近亲人、敬重大臣、体恤群臣、对待庶民如同儿子、招揽各种工匠、优待远来之人、安抚诸侯。修身则道就能确立，尊重贤者就没有困惑，亲近亲人则父辈和兄弟们没有怨言，敬重大臣则不会迷乱，体恤群臣则士人的报答之礼就会重，对待庶民如同儿子就会使百姓得到激励，招揽各种工匠就会使得财物充足，优待远来之人就会四方归顺，安抚诸侯就会天下敬畏。整洁得穿着盛装，不合礼的不动，这是用来修身的；摒去谗言，远离女色，轻视财货而看重德性，这是用来激励贤者的；尊奉爵位，厚待俸禄，与他们同一好恶，这是用来激励亲人的；属官盛多足以任使，这是用以激励大臣的；对之忠信而加厚俸禄，这是用以激励士人的；徭役不违农时，薄收赋税，这是用以激励百姓的；每天检查，每月考核，根据所做之事给予俸禄，这是用以激励各种工匠的；欢迎和礼送外来之人，奖励善良的人而哀怜能力差的人，这是用以优待远方来人的；延续绝嗣之人，重建灭亡之国，评定乱局，扶持危弱的国家，让诸侯按时来朝见，赐予之物丰厚而贡献之物要少，这是用以安抚诸侯的。

治理天下国家总共有九条原则，用来施行的途径只有一个。凡做事情，预先有了准备就能顺利，没有准备就会失败。言语提前有准备就不会有窒碍，做事提前有准备就不会困顿，行动提前有准备就不会出问题，做人之道提前有准备就不会穷途。在下位之人得不到上位人的信任，就不能治理百姓。获得上位人的信任有途径，不得到朋友的信任就不能得到上位人的信任。得到朋友的信任有途径，不孝顺父母亲，就不能得到朋友的信任。孝顺双亲有途径，反省自身，如果不诚，就不孝顺双亲。诚身有途径，不明白善，就不能诚身。

　　诚是天之道，做到诚，是人之道。诚，就是不用勉强而不偏不倚，不用思虑而得当，从容地符合中庸之道，这就是圣人。做到诚，就是选择善而坚定地持守，广泛地学习、仔细地探问、谨慎地思考、明白地辨析、笃实地践履。要么不学，学了就不能不坚持。要么不问，问了就不能不坚持；要么不思考，思考了就不能不坚持；要么不辨析，辨析了就不得不坚持；要么不践行，践行了就不得不坚持。别人能做到一次，我要做到一百次；别人能做到十次，我做到一千次。如果能照这个途径去做，那么，即使是愚昧的人也一定会变得聪明，即使是柔弱的人也一定会变得刚强。

　　【英译】The Duke Ai asked about government. The Master said, "The government of Wen and Wu is displayed in the records, ——the tablets of wood and bamboo. Let there be the men and the government will flourish; but without the men, their government decays and ceases. With the right men the growth of government is rapid, just as vegetation is rapid in the earth; and, moreover, their government might be called an easily-growing rush. Therefore the administration of government lies in getting proper men. Such men are to be got by means of the ruler's own character. That character is to be cultivated by his treading in the ways of duty. And the treading those ways of duty is to be cultivated by the cherishing of benevolence. Benevolence is the characteristic element of humanity, and the great exercise of it is in loving relatives. Righteousness is the accordance of actions with what is right, and the great exercise of it is in honoring the worthy. The decreasing measures of the love due to relatives, and the steps in the honor due to the worthy, are produced by the principle of propriety. When those in inferior situations do not possess the confidence of their superiors, they cannot retain the government of the people. Hence the sovereign may not neglect the cultivation of his own character. Wishing to cultivate his character, he may not neglect to serve his parents. In order to serve his parents, he may not neglect to acquire knowledge of men. In order to know men, he may not dispense with a knowledge of Heaven. ”

The duties of universal obligation are five and the virtues wherewith they are practiced are three. The duties are those between sovereign and minister, between father and son, between husband and wife, between elder brother and younger, and those belonging to the intercourse of friends. Those five are the duties of universal obligation. Knowledge, magnanimity, and energy, these three, are the virtues universally binding. And the means by which they carry the duties into practice is singleness. Some are born with the knowledge of those duties; some know them by study; and some acquire the knowledge after a painful feeling of their ignorance. But the knowledge being possessed, it comes to the same thing. Some practice them with a natural ease; some from a desire for their advantages; and some by strenuous effort. But the achievement being made, it comes to the same thing. The Master said, “To be fond of learning is to be near to knowledge. To practice with vigor is to be near to magnanimity. To possess the feeling of shame is to be near to energy. He who knows these three things, knows how to cultivate his own character. Knowing how to cultivate his own character, he knows how to govern other men. Knowing how to govern other men, he knows how to govern the kingdom with all its states and families. ”

All who have the government of the kingdom with its states and families have nine standard rules to follow; —viz. the cultivation of their own characters the honoring of men of virtue and talents; affection towards their relatives; respect towards the great ministers; kind and considerate treatment of the whole body of officers; dealing with the mass of the people as children; encouraging the resort of all classes of artisans; indulgent treatment of men from a distance; and the kindly cherishing of the princes of the States. By the ruler's cultivation of his own character, the duties of universal obligation are set forth. By honoring men of virtue and talents, he is preserved from errors of judgment. By showing affection to his relatives, there is no grumbling nor resentment among his uncles and brethren. By respecting the great ministers, he is kept from errors in the practice of government. By kind and considerate treatment of the whole body of officers, they are led to make the most grateful return for his courtesies. By dealing with the mass of the people as his children, they are led to exhort one another to what is good. By encouraging the resort of an classes of artisans, his resources for expenditure are rendered ample. By indulgent treatment of men from a distance, they are brought to resort to him from all quarters. And by kindly cherishing the princes of the States, the whole kingdom is brought to revere him. Self-adjustment and purification, with careful regulation of his dress, and the not making a movement contrary to the rules of propriety: —this is the way for a ruler to cultivate his person. Discarding slanderers, and keeping himself from the seductions of beauty; making light of riches, and giving honor to virtue: —this is the way for him to encourage men of worth and talents. Giving them places of honor and large emolument. and sharing with them in their likes and dislikes: —this is the way for him to encourage his relatives to love him. Giving them numerous officers to discharge their orders and commissions：—this is the way for him to encourage the great ministers. According to them a generous confidence，and making their emoluments large：—this is the way to encourage the body of officers. Employing them only at the proper times，and making the imposts light：—this is the way to encourage the people. By daily examinations and monthly trials，and by making their rations in accordance with their labors：—this is the way to encourage the classes of artisans. To escort them on their departure and meet them on their coming；to commend the good among them，and show compassion to the incompetent：—this is the way to treat indulgently men from a distance. To restore families whose line of succession has been broken，and to revive States that have been extinguished；to reduce to order states that are in confusion，and support those which are in peril；to have fixed times for their own reception at court，and the reception of their envoys；to send them away after liberal treatment，and welcome their coming with small contributions：—this is the way to cherish the princes of the States.

　　All who have the government of the kingdom with its States and families have the above nine standard rules. And the means by which they are carried into practice is singleness. In all things success depends on previous preparation，and without such previous preparation there is sure to be failure. If what is to be spoken be previously determined，there will be no stumbling. If affairs be previously determined，there will be no difficulty with them. If one's actions have been previously determined，there will be no sorrow in connection with them. If principles of conduct have been previously determined，the practice of them will be inexhaustible. When those in inferior situations do not obtain the confidence of the sovereign, they cannot succeed in governing the people. There is a way to obtain the confidence of the sovereign; —if one is not trusted by his friends, he will not get the confidence of his sovereign. There is a way to being trusted by one's friends; —if one is not obedient to his parents, he will not be true to friends. There is a way to being obedient to one's parents; —if one, on turning his thoughts in upon himself, finds a want of sincerity, he will not be obedient to his parents. There is a way to the attainment of sincerity in one's self; —if a man do not understand what is good, he will not attain sincerity in himself.

Sincerity is the way of Heaven. The attainment of sincerity is the way of men. He who possesses sincerity is he who, without an effort, hits what is right, and apprehends, without the exercise of thought; — he is the sage who naturally and easily embodies the right way. He who attains to sincerity is he who chooses what is good, and firmly holds it fast. To this attainment there are requisite the extensive study of what is good, accurate inquiry about it, careful reflection on it, the clear discrimination of it, and the earnest practice of it. The superior man, while there is anything he has not studied, or while in what he has studied there is anything he cannot understand, will not intermit his labor. While there is anything he has not inquired about, or anything in what he has inquired about which he does not know, he will not intermit his labor. While there is anything which he has not reflected on, or anything in what he has reflected on which he does not apprehend, he will not intermit his labor. While there is anything which he has not discriminated or his discrimination is not clear, he will not intermit his labor. If there be anything which he has not practiced, or his practice fails in earnestness，he will not intermit his labor. If another man succeed by one effort，he will use a hundred efforts. If another man succeed by ten efforts，he will use a thousand. Let a man proceed in this way，and，though dull，he will surely become intelligent；though weak，he will surely become strong.

【注释】

[1]"仁"，理雅各翻译为"benevolence"，辜鸿铭、林语堂翻译为"moral sense"，陈荣捷翻译为"humanity"，安乐哲、郝大维翻译为"authoritative conduct"。理雅各的翻译侧重于"仁慈"，虽然包含在"仁"的含义中，但并不是它的根本含义。辜鸿铭和林语堂的翻译侧重于"仁"的道德含义，而安乐哲、郝大维的翻译侧重于文本中的"仁"作为当权者行为的一面。从"仁者，人也"出发，陈荣捷的翻译较为合适，其他的翻译也能作为了解"仁"的不同渠道。

[2]"义"，理雅各、陈荣捷翻译为"righteousness"，辜鸿铭、林语堂翻译为"the sense of justice"，安乐哲、郝大维翻译为"appropriateness"。理雅各和陈荣捷的翻译有着"正义"的维度，辜鸿铭和林语堂的翻译侧重个人的感受，安乐哲、郝大维的翻译则侧重于"合适"。考虑到"义"所具有的公共维度及其与"宜"的区别，理雅各和陈荣捷的翻译较为合适。

[3]"知"，理雅各翻译为"knowledge"，林语堂、陈荣捷和安乐哲、郝大维翻译为"wisdom"，辜鸿铭翻译为"intelligence"。"knowledge"侧重于知识，"intelligence"侧重于智力、智能，"wisdom"侧重于智慧，更加符合文义。

[4]"诚"，理雅各、陈荣捷翻译为"sincerity"，辜鸿铭、林语堂翻译为"truth"，安乐哲、郝大维翻译为"creativity"。"sincerity"侧重于个人的心境之"诚"，"truth"侧重于知识层面，"creativity"侧重天道的客观层面。综合而言，"creativity"的翻译更能贴合"天道"的原始含义，但仍旧有所不足，因为"诚"是对天道之"生生"的描述而不是指称。

第二十一章

【原文】自诚明[1]，谓之性；自明诚，谓之教。诚则明矣，明则诚矣。

【译文】从诚而实现明，这是本性的作用；从明实现诚，这是教化的作用。做到诚，就能够明；做到明，就能够诚。

【英译】When we have intelligence resulting from sincerity，this condition is to be ascribed to nature；when we have sincerity resulting from intelligence，this condition is to be ascribed to instruction. But given the sincerity，and there shall be the intelligence；given the intelligence，and there shall be the sincerity.

【注释】

[1] "明"，理雅各、辜鸿铭翻译为 "intelligence"，林语堂翻译为 "understanding"，陈荣捷翻译为 "enlightenment"，安乐哲、郝大维也翻译为 "understanding"。考虑到 "明" 所需要的教化和学习过程，"understanding" 更为恰当。

第二十二章

【原文】唯天下至诚，为能尽其性；能尽其性，则能尽人之性；能尽人之性，则能尽物之性；能尽物之性，则可以赞天地之化育；可以赞天地之化育，则可以与天地参矣。[1]

【译文】只有天下至诚之人，才能够充分实现自身之性；能够充分实现自身之性，就能够充分实现他人之性；能够充分实现他人之性，就能够充分实现物之性；能够充分实现物之性，就能够参与天地之间万物的生成；能够参与天地之间万物的生成，就可以与天地之道并列为三。

【英译】It is only he who is possessed of the most complete sincerity that can exist under heaven，who can give its full development to his nature. Able to give its full development to his own nature，he can do the same to the nature of other men. Able to give its full development to the nature of other men，he can give their full development to the natures of animals and things. Able to give their full development to the natures of creatures and things，he can assist the transforming and nourishing powers of Heaven and Earth. Able to assist the transforming and nourishing powers of Heaven and Earth，he may with Heaven and Earth form a ternion.

【注释】

[1] "与天地参"，理雅各、陈荣捷分别使用了 "ternion" 和 "trinity"，侧重于 "三" 的含义。林语堂翻译为 "the equals of heaven and earth"，安乐哲、郝大维翻译为 "take their place as members of this triad"，侧重于人道和天道、地道平等的含义。这两者翻译结合起来能够较为合适地说明 "参" 的含义。而辜鸿铭使用了 "with the Powers of the Universe"，也将 "尽物之性" 翻译为 "get to the bottom of the laws of physical nature"，这样就偏离了文本的字面含义。

第二十三章

【原文】其次致曲，曲能有诚，诚则形，形则著，著则明，明则动，动则变，变则化，唯天下至诚为能化。[1]

【译文】圣人之下的人，可以在局部和小事中推致，在局部和小事中实现诚，诚就能在外部表现出来，在外部表现出来就会很显著，显著就会昭明，昭明就会感动他人，感动他人就会使其发生变化，只有天下至诚之人会使他人发生变化。

【英译】Next to the above is he who cultivates to the utmost the shoots of goodness in him. From those he can attain to the possession of sincerity. This sincerity becomes apparent. From being apparent，it becomes manifest. From being manifest，it becomes brilliant. Brilliant, it affects others. Affecting others，they are changed by it. Changed by it，they are transformed. It is only he who is possessed of the most complete sincerity that can exist under heaven，who can transform.

【注释】

[1]"曲、形、著、明、动、变、化"，理雅各使用了"shoots, apparent, manifest, brilliant, affect, changed, transformed"，辜鸿铭使用了"particular, substance, reality, intelligence, power, influence, creative power"，林语堂使用了"particular, expression, evidence, clarity or luminosity, activate, power, influence"，陈荣捷使用了"particular, expression, conspicuous, clear, move, change, transform"，安乐哲、郝大维使用了"aspect, determinate, manifest, understanding, affected, change, transformed"。其中，辜鸿铭使用的"substance"和"reality"等稍微偏离了文本，而"power"所蕴含的"权力""力量"等含义与圣人之化有所区别，故而理雅各、陈荣捷和安乐哲、郝大维的翻译比较恰当。

第二十四章

【原文】至诚之道，可以前知。国家将兴，必有祯祥；国家将亡，必有妖孽；见乎蓍龟，动乎四体。祸福将至：善，必先知之；不善，必先知之。故至诚如神。[1]

【译文】掌握至诚之道，可以预知未来。国家将要兴盛，必然有吉兆；国家将要灭亡，必然有妖孽，表现在卜筮时的蓍草和龟甲之上，活动在人们的四肢中。祸福将要到来，好的一定能预先知晓，不好的也一定预先知晓。因此至诚之人如同神明。

【英译】It is characteristic of the most entire sincerity to be able to foreknow. When a nation or family is about to flourish，there are sure to be happy omens；and when it is about to perish，there are sure to be unlucky omens. Such events are seen in the milfoil and tortoise，and affect the movements of the four limbs. When calamity or happiness is about to come，the good shall certainly be foreknown by him，and the evil also. Therefore the individual possessed of the most complete sincerity is like a spirit.

【注释】

[1] "神"，理雅各翻译为"spirit"，林语堂翻译为"celestial spirit"，辜鸿铭翻译为"spiritual being"，陈荣捷翻译为"spirit"，安乐哲、郝大维翻译为"numinous"。这里的"神"与"spirit"有所差别，安乐哲、郝大维的翻译较为恰当。

第二十五章

【原文】诚者自成也，而道自道也。诚者物之终始，不诚无物。是故君子诚之为贵。诚者非自成己而已也，所以成物也。成己，仁也；成物，知也。性之德也，合外内之道也，故时措之宜也。

【译文】诚是人自己成就的，道是人自己践履的。诚贯穿万物的开始和终结，没有诚就没有万物。因此君子以诚为贵。诚并不是自己成就自己，也是成就事物。成就自己，是仁；成就事物，是智。（诚）是性之德，是内外相合之道，因此随时应用都能适宜。

【英译】Sincerity is that whereby self-completion is effected，and its way is that by which man must direct himself. Sincerity is the end and beginning of things；without sincerity there would be nothing. On this account，the superior man regards the attainment of sincerity as the most excellent thing. The possessor of sincerity does not merely accomplish the self-completion of himself. With this quality he completes other men and things also. The completing himself shows his perfect virtue. The completing other men and things shows his knowledge. Both these are virtues belonging to the nature，and this is the way by which a union is effected of the external and internal. Therefore，whenever he—the entirely sincere man—employs them，—that is，these virtues, their action will be right.

第二十六章

【原文】故至诚无息。不息则久，久则征，征则悠远，悠远则博厚，博厚则高明。博厚，所以载物也；高明，所以覆物也；悠久，所以成物也。博厚配地，高明配天，悠久无疆。如此者，不见而章，不动而变，无为而成。天地之道，可一言而尽也：其为物不贰，则其生物不测。天地之道：博也，厚也，高也，明也，悠也，久也。今夫天，斯昭昭之多，及其无穷也，日月星辰系焉，万物覆焉。今夫地，一撮土之多，及其广厚，载华岳而不重，振河海而不泄，万物载焉。今夫山，一卷石之多，及其广大，草木生之，禽兽居之，宝藏兴焉。今夫水，一勺之多，及其不测，鼋鼍、蛟龙、鱼鳖生焉，货财殖焉。诗云："维天之命，於穆不已！"盖曰天之所以为天也。"於乎不显！文王之德之纯！"盖曰文王之所以为文也，纯亦不已。

【译文】因此至诚是不休止的。不休止则持久，持久则表现出来，表现出来则悠长久远，悠长久远就能广博深厚，广博深厚就能高大光明。广博深厚能承载万物，高大光明能覆盖万物，悠长久远能成就万物。广博深厚与地相配，高大光明与天相配，悠长久远而无边界。这样的至诚，看不见但很显著，不运动但能产生变化，不作为但能成就万物。天地之道可以用一句话说明白：它自身不二，于是生成万物也不可测量。天地之道博、厚、高、明、悠、久。现在说天，就是有光亮的这部分之多，及其到无穷处，日月星辰都系缚其上，万物都被它覆盖。现在说地，就是一撮土这么多，及其广厚之处，承载华山而不觉得重，收容河海而不泄露，承载着万物。现在说山，就是这么些石头，及其广大之处，草木生长其间，禽兽居住其间，宝藏在其中兴盛。现在说水，有一勺这么多，及其不可测量，鼋鼍、蛟龙、鱼鳖生长其中，货财在里面繁殖。《诗经》说："天之所命，深远而不停歇。"这就是天之所以成为天的原因。"这岂不很明显，文王之德纯一不杂。"这就是周文王之所以为文王的原因，纯一而且不停息。

【英译】Hence to entire sincerity there belongs ceaselessness. Not ceasing, it continues long. Continuing long, it evidences itself. Evidencing itself, it reaches far. Reaching far, it becomes large and substantial. Large and substantial, it becomes high and brilliant. Large and substantial；—this is how it contains all things. High and brilliant；—this is how it overspreads all things. Reaching far and continuing long；—this is how it perfects all things. So large and substantial, the individual possessing it is the co-equal of Earth. So high and brilliant, it makes him the co-equal of Heaven. So far-reaching and long-continuing, it makes him infinite. Such being its nature, without any display, it becomes manifested；without any movement, it produces changes；and without any effort, it accomplishes its ends. The way of Heaven and Earth may be completely declared in one sentence. They are without any doubleness，and so they produce things in a manner that is unfathomable. The way of Heaven and Earth is large and substantial, high and brilliant, far-reaching and long-enduring. The Heaven now before us is only this bright shining spot; but when viewed in its inexhaustible extent, the sun, moon, stars, and constellations of the zodiac, are suspended in it, and all things are overspread by it. The earth before us is but a handful of soil; but when regarded in its breadth and thickness, it sustains mountains like the Hwa and the Yo, without feeling their weight, and contains the rivers and seas, without their leaking away. The mountain now before us appears only a stone; but when contemplated in all the vastness of its size, we see how the grass and trees are produced on it, and birds and beasts dwell on it, and precious things which men treasure up are found on it. The water now before us appears but a ladleful; yet extending our view to its unfathomable depths, the largest tortoises, iguanas, iguanodons, dragons, fishes, and turtles, are produced in it, articles of value and sources of wealth abound in it. It is said in the Book of Poetry, "The ordinances of Heaven, how profound are they and unceasing!" The meaning is, that it is thus that Heaven is Heaven. And again, "How illustrious was it, the singleness of the virtue of King Wen!" indicating that it was thus that King Wen was what he was. Singleness likewise is unceasing.

第二十七章

【原文】大哉圣人之道! 洋洋乎! 发育万物,峻极于天。优优大哉! 礼仪三百,威仪三千。待其人而后行。故曰苟不至德,至道不凝焉。故君子尊德性而道问学,致广大而尽精微,极高明而道中庸。温故而知新，敦厚以崇礼。是故居上不骄，为下不倍，国有道其言足以兴，国无道其默足以容。诗曰"既明且哲，以保其身"，其此之谓与！

【译文】伟大啊圣人之道！广大呀！生成和养育万物，与天一样高大。悠悠大哉！大的礼仪有三百，小的礼节有三千，等待适合之人出现才能推行。因此说，若无有至德之人，则至道就不会形成。因此君子要尊奉德性并由学问引导，致力于广大之事而能发挥其精微之义，达到高明的境地而又遵循中庸之道。温习已经掌握的知识而获取新知，加厚自己已有的能力以崇尚礼。因此，君子身居上位不骄矜，在下位不悖逆。如果国家有道，它的言谈足以振兴国家；如果国家无道，他的沉默足以保全自身。《诗经》说"既聪明又睿智，能够保全自身"，大概说的就是这个意思吧。

【英译】How great is the path proper to the Sage! Like overflowing water, it sends forth and nourishes all things, and rises up to the height of heaven. All complete is its greatness! It embraces the three hundred rules of ceremony, and the three thousand rules of demeanor. It waits for the proper man, and then it is trodden. Hence it is said, "Only by perfect virtue can the perfect path, in all its courses, be made a fact." Therefore, the superior man honors his virtuous nature, and maintains constant inquiry and study, seeking to carry it out to its breadth and greatness, so as to omit none of the more exquisite and minute points which it embraces, and to raise it to its greatest height and brilliancy, so as to pursue the course of the Mean. He cherishes his old knowledge, and is continually acquiring new. He exerts an honest, generous earnestness, in the esteem and practice of all propriety. Thus, when occupying a high situation he is not proud, and in a low situation he is not insubordinate. When the kingdom is well governed, he is sure by his words to rise；and when it is ill—governed，he is sure by his silence to command forbearance to himself. Is not this what we find in the Book of Poetry，— "Intelligent is he and prudent，and so preserves his person？"

第二十八章

【原文】子曰："愚而好自用，贱而好自专，生乎今之世，反古之道。如此者，裁及其身者也。"非天子，不议礼，不制度，不考文。今天下车同轨，书同文，行同伦。虽有其位，苟无其德，不敢作礼乐焉；虽有其德，苟无其位，亦不敢作礼乐焉。子曰："吾说夏礼，杞不足征也；吾学殷礼，有宋存焉；吾学周礼，今用之，吾从周。"

【译文】孔子说："愚昧而好刚愎自用，卑贱而好独断专行，生于现在的时代，却要返回古代的道路，像这样的人，灾祸就要降到他的身上了。"不是天子，就不议定礼仪，不创制法度，不考定书名。如今天下车轮的距离相同，文字相同，行为伦理相同。虽然身有天子之位，如果没有圣人之德，是不敢制礼作乐的；虽然有圣人之德，如果没有天子之位，也同样是不敢制礼作乐的。孔子说："我想说夏代的礼制，可是在杞国得不到验证；我学习殷商的礼制，如今还有宋国存在；我学习周朝的礼制，今天仍旧在使用，所以我遵从周礼。"

【英译】The Master said，"Let a man who is ignorant be fond of using his own judgment；let a man without rank be fond of assuming a directing power to himself；let a man who is living in the present age go back to the ways of antiquity；—on the persons of all who act thus calamities will be sure to come." To no one but the Son of Heaven does it belong to order ceremonies，to fix the measures，and to determine the written characters. Now over the kingdom，carriages have all wheels of the same size；all writing is with the same characters；and for conduct there are the same rules. One may occupy the throne，but if he have not the proper virtue，he may not dare to make ceremonies or music. One may have the virtue，but if he do not occupy the throne，he may not presume to make ceremonies or music. The Master said，"I may describe the ceremonies of the Xia dynasty，but Qi cannot sufficiently attest my words. I have learned the ceremonies of the Yin dynasty，and in Song they still continue. I have learned the ceremonies of Zhou，which are now used，and I follow Zhou."

第二十九章

【原文】王天下有三重焉，其寡过矣乎！上焉者虽善无征，无征不信，不信民弗从；下焉者虽善不尊，不尊不信，不信民弗从。故君子之道：本诸身，征诸庶民，考诸三王而不缪，建诸天地而不悖，质诸鬼神而无疑，百世以俟圣人而不惑。是故君子动而世为天下道，行而世为天下法，言而世为天下则。远之则有望，近之则不厌。诗曰："在彼无恶，在此无射；庶几夙夜，以永终誉！"君子未有不如此而蚤有誉于天下者也。

【译文】称王于天下有三件大事（议礼，制度，考文），做到了就会有很少的过错。在上位的人虽然良善，但没有征验，而没有征验就不能取信，不能取信则百姓就不服从了。身在下位的人虽然良善，但自己地位不尊崇，也就不能取信，不能取信于民，百姓也就不肯服从了。因此君子之道，要以修身为本，在庶民中获得验证，考查于三王之礼而无谬误，建立后不违背天地之道，质问于鬼神而无疑虑，百世之后的圣人也不会对此有疑惑。因此君子的动作能够世代为天下之法则，行动能够世代为天下之法度，言论能够世代为天下的准则。远离君子的人希望能靠近，靠近君子的人不会厌倦。《诗经》说："在那边没有怨恨，在这里没有厌倦。希望早起晚睡，以便永远保持声誉。"君子从没有不这样做而能早有声誉于天下的。

【英译】He who attains to the sovereignty of the kingdom, having those three important things, shall be able to effect that there shall be few errors under his government. However excellent may have been the regulations of those of former times, they cannot be attested. Not being attested, they cannot command credence, and not being credited, the people would not follow them. However excellent might be the regulations made by one in an inferior situation, he is not in a position to be honored. Unhonored, he cannot command credence, and not being credited, the people would not follow his rules. Therefore the institutions of the Ruler are rooted in his own character and conduct, and sufficient attestation of them is given by the masses of the people. He examines them by comparison with those of the three kings, and finds them without mistake. He sets them up before Heaven and Earth, and finds nothing in them contrary to their mode of operation. He presents himself with them before spiritual beings, and no doubts about them arise. He is prepared to wait for the rise of a sage a hundred ages after, and has no misgivings. His presenting himself with his institutions before spiritual beings, without any doubts arising about them, shows that he knows Heaven. His being prepared, without any misgivings, to wait for the rise of a sage a hundred ages after, shows that he knows men. Such being the case, the movements of such a ruler, illustrating his institutions, constitute an example to the world for ages. His acts are for ages a law to the kingdom. His words are for ages a lesson to the kingdom. Those who are far from him，look longingly for him；and those who are near him are never wearied with him. It is said in the Book of Poetry，— "Not disliked there，not tired of here，from day to day and night to night，will they perpetuate their praise." Never has there been a ruler，who did not realize this description，that obtained an early renown throughout the kingdom.

第 三 十 章

【原文】仲尼祖述尧舜，宪章文武；上律天时，下袭水土。辟如天地之无不持载，无不覆帱，辟如四时之错行，如日月之代明。万物并育而不相害，道并行而不相悖，小德川流，大德敦化，此天地之所以为大也。[1]

【译文】孔子继承遥远的尧舜之道，效法周文王和武王的法度，上效法天地自然变化之则，下因循水土一定之理。如同天地那样无不维持承载、无不覆盖遮护，如同四季交替而行，如同日月交替而明。万物共同生长发育而不相害，各种道理并行而不相违背，小的德性如同河水不息地流动，大的德性如同万物之生化，这就是天地之所以为大的原因。

【英译】Zhong-ni handed down the doctrines of Yao and Shun，as if they had been his ancestors，and elegantly displayed the regulations of Wen and Wu，taking them as his model. Above，he harmonized with the times of Heaven，and below，he was conformed to the water and land. He may be compared to Heaven and Earth in their supporting and containing，their overshadowing and curtaining，all things. He may be compared to the four seasons in their alternating progress，and to the sun and moon in their successive shining. All things are nourished together without their injuring one another. The courses of the seasons， and of the sun and moon，are pursued without any collision among them. The smaller energies are like river currents；the greater energies are seen in mighty transformations. It is this which makes heaven and earth so great.

【注释】

[1] "大德"和"小德"之"德"，理雅各翻译为"energy"，安乐哲、郝大维翻译为"excellences"，辜鸿铭、林语堂、陈荣捷翻译为"forces"。从文本含义出发，安乐哲、郝大维的翻译更能贴合"德"的内涵。

第三十一章

【原文】 唯天下至圣，为能聪明睿知，足以有临也；宽裕温柔，足以有容也；发强刚毅，足以有执也；齐庄中正，足以有敬也；文理密察，足以有别也。溥博渊泉，而时出之。溥博如天，渊泉如渊。见而民莫不敬，言而民莫不信，行而民莫不说。是以声名洋溢乎中国，施及蛮貊；舟车所至，人力所通；天之所覆，地之所载，日月所照，霜露所队；凡有血气者，莫不尊亲，故曰配天。

【译文】 只有天下至圣之人，才能做到聪明智慧，足以治理百姓；宽裕温柔，足以包容天下；奋发刚毅，足以执掌国家；端庄中正，足以有敬畏之姿；思维缜密而明察，足以辨别是非。（圣人）广博如深泉，应时表现于外；广博得如同天空，静沉得如同深渊。见到他，百姓没有不崇敬的，他的言论百姓没有不听信的，他的行为百姓没有不感到快乐的。因此他的声明洋溢于中国，传播到蛮貊之地，传播到船和车等人力所能到达的地方，传播到天之所覆盖、地之所载持、日月之所照临，霜露之所降落的地方，凡是有血气的人都尊奉和亲近他，因此说圣人与天相配。

【英译】 It is only he，possessed of all sagely qualities that can exist under heaven，who shows himself quick in apprehension，clear in discernment，of farreaching intelligence，and all-embracing knowledge，fitted to exercise rule；magnanimous，generous，benign，and mild，fitted to exercise forbearance；impulsive，energetic，firm，and enduring，fitted to maintain a firm hold；self-adjusted，grave，never swerving from the Mean，and correct，fitted to command reverence；accomplished，distinctive，concentrative，and searching，fitted to exercise discrimination. All-embracing is he and vast，deep and active as a fountain，sending forth in their due season his virtues. All-embracing and vast，he is like Heaven. Deep and active as a fountain，he is like the abyss. He is seen，and the people all reverence him；he speaks，and the people all believe him；he acts，and the people all are pleased with him. Therefore his fame overspreads the Middle Kingdom，and extends to all barbarous tribes. Wherever ships and carriages reach；wherever the strength of man penetrates；wherever the heavens overshadow and the earth sustains；wherever the sun and moon shine；wherever frosts and dews fall：—all who have blood and breath unfeignedly honor and love him. Hence it is said，"He is the equal of Heaven."

第三十二章

【原文】唯天下至诚，为能经纶天下之大经，立天下之大本，知天地之化育。夫焉有所倚？肫肫其仁！渊渊其渊！浩浩其天！苟不固聪明圣知达天德者，其孰能知之？

【译文】只有天下至诚之人，才能经理天下的根本大法，确立天下的根本之道，知晓天地的化育之功，这样怎能有其他依仗呢？他的仁如此挚恳，如同深渊那样不可测度，如同天那样浩大。如果不是的确聪明睿智而通达天德的人，谁又能够理解他呢？

【英译】It is only the individual possessed of the most entire sincerity that can exist under Heaven，who can adjust the great invariable relations of mankind，establish the great fundamental virtues of humanity，and know the transforming and nurturing operations of Heaven and Earth；-shall this individual have any being or anything beyond himself on which he depends？Call him man in his ideal，how earnest is he！Call him an abyss，how deep is he！Call him Heaven，how vast is he！Who can know him，but he who is indeed quick in apprehension，clear in discernment，of far-reaching intelligence，and all-embracing knowledge，possessing all Heavenly virtue？

第三十三章

【原文】诗曰"衣锦尚䌹"，恶其文之著也。故君子之道，暗然而日章；小人之道，的然而日亡。君子之道：淡而不厌，简而文，温而理，知远之近，知风之自，知微之显，可与入德矣。诗云："潜虽伏矣，亦孔之昭！"故君子内省不疚，无恶于志。君子之所不可及者，其唯人之所不见乎。诗云："相在尔室，尚不愧于屋漏。"故君子不动而敬，不言而信。诗曰："奏假无言，时靡有争。"是故君子不赏而民劝，不怒而民威于铁钺。诗曰："不显惟德！百辟其刑之。"是故君子笃恭而天下平。诗云："予怀明德，不大声以色。"子曰："声色之于以化民，末也。"诗曰："德辖如毛"，毛犹有伦。"上天之载，无声无臭"，至矣！

【译文】《诗经》说"穿着锦衣时候外面要覆盖单衣"，这是厌恶锦服的文色过于华丽。因此君子之道，暗淡但日益彰明，小人之道鲜明但日渐消亡。君子之道，清淡而令人不厌，简朴而有文理，温和而有秩序，知道远是从近开始的，知道风来自何处，知道隐微会走向显著，这样，可以拥有德性。《诗经》说："虽然深入水底隐藏，但也被看得很清楚。"所以，君子反省自己而没有内疚，也就无愧于志向了。君子之所以不可企及的地方，大概就在这种别人看不见的地方吧！《诗经》说："看你独处室中时，应当无愧于西北角的神明。"因此君子不动时也能使人敬畏，不说话时也能使人信任。《诗经》说："祷告时无人出声，没有争执。"因此君子不用赏赐而百姓受到吸引，不发怒而百姓敬畏其威严胜于斧钺。《诗经》说："文王的德性非常显著，诸侯都来效法。"因此君子笃实恭敬而天下太平。《诗经》说："我怀念文王的明德，不疾声厉色。"孔子说："疾声厉色以教化百姓，是最末等的。"《诗经》说："德性犹如羽毛"，但毛仍有与他能相比的。"上天承载万物，无声无味"，这就是最高的。

【英译】It is said in the Book of Poetry, "Over her embroidered robe she puts a plain single garment," intimating a dislike to the display of the elegance of the former. Just so, it is the way of the superior man to prefer the concealment of his virtue, while it daily becomes more illustrious, and it is the way of the mean man to seek notoriety, while he daily goes more and more to ruin. It is characteristic of the superior man, appearing insipid, yet never to produce satiety；while showing a simple negligence, yet to have his accomplishments recognized；while seemingly plain, yet to be discriminating. He knows how what is distant lies in what is near. He knows where the wind proceeds from. He knows how what is minute becomes manifested. Such a one, we may be sure, will enter into virtue. It is said in the Book of Poetry, "Although the fish sink and lie at the bottom, it is still quite clearly seen." Therefore the superior man examines his heart, that there may be nothing wrong there, and that he may have no cause for dissatisfaction with himself. That wherein the superior man cannot be equaled is simply this, —his work which other men cannot see. It is said in the Book of Poetry, "Looked at in your apartment, be there free from shame as being exposed to the light of Heaven." Therefore, the superior man, even when he is not moving, has a feeling of reverence, and while he speaks not, he has the feeling of truthfulness. It is said in the Book of Poetry, "In silence is the offering presented, and the spirit approached to; there is not the slightest contention." Therefore the superior man does not use rewards, and the people are stimulated to virtue. He does not show anger, and the people are awed more than by hatchets and battle-axes. It is said in the Book of Poetry, "What needs no display is virtue. All the princes imitate it." Therefore, the superior man being sincere and reverential, the whole world is conducted to a state of happy tranquility. It is said in the Book of Poetry, "I regard with pleasure your brilliant virtue, making no great display of itself in sounds and appearances." The Master said, "Among the appliances to transform the people, sound and appearances are but trivial influences". It is said in another ode, "His Virtue is light as a hair." Still, a hair will admit of comparison as to its size. "The doings of the supreme Heaven have neither sound nor smell." That is perfect virtue.

后　记

　　《大学》和《中庸》原本是《礼记》中的章节，自唐、宋以来逐渐受到学者的重视，成为儒学的核心经典，即"四书"中的两部。同时，《大学》和《中庸》自清末以来被翻译为各种文字，成为海外学者了解中华文化的重要窗口。本次注译，在中文材料方面主要选取了郑玄、朱熹和王夫之的相关解释，希望能彰显《大学》《中庸》在历代思想家那里的差异化理解；在英文方面，选取了理雅各（James Legge）、辜鸿铭、林语堂、陈荣捷、安乐哲（Roger T. Ames）的翻译进行比较，希望能表现更多维度的诠释空间。考虑到版权问题，本书选取了理雅各的翻译为全文英译以供参考。理雅各的译本出版于19世纪六七十年代，所用英文的文法和词汇与现今有所差异，望读者明察。本书所用书目版本如下：

　　郑玄：《礼记注》，王锷点校，中华书局2021年版。

　　朱熹：《四书章句集注》，中华书局1983年版。

　　王夫之：《四书训义》《读四书大全说》，岳麓书社2011年版。

　　[英] James Leges［理雅各］编译：《中国经典》（上），华东师范大学出版社2010年版。

　　王京涛述评：《大学 中庸》，辜鸿铭英译，中华书局2017年版。

　　林语堂：《孔子的智慧》（*The Wisdom of Confucius*），外语教学与研究出版社2009年版。

　　A SOURCE BOOK IN CHINESE PHILOSOPHY, Translated and

Compiled by WING-TSIT CHAN（陈荣捷），Princeton University Press，1963.

　　[美] Roger T.Ames（安乐哲）、[美] David L.Hall（郝大维）：《切中伦常：〈中庸〉的新诠与新译》，彭国翔译，中国社会科学出版社2011年版。

　　[美] Roger T.Ames（安乐哲）：《先秦儒家哲学文献译解》，商务印书馆2023年版。

段重阳

西元2023年8月20日于济南